SPIRITUAL WARFARE FOR THE WOUNDED

Spiritual Warfare for the Wounded

Dr. Mark Johnson

Servant Publications
Ann Arbor, Michigan

Vine Books is an imprint of Servant Publications especially
designed to serve Evangelical Christians.

Published by Servant Publications
P.O. Box 8617
Ann Arbor, Michigan 48107

Cover design by Michael Andaloro

93 94 95 96 10 9 8 7 6 5 4 3

Printed in the United States of America

ISBN 0-89283-753-5

Library of Congress Cataloging-in-Publication Data
Johnson, Mark.
Spiritual warfare for the wounded / Mark Johnson.
p. cm.
ISBN 0-89283-753-5
1. Spiritual warfare. 2. Adult child abuse victims—Religious life.
I. Title.
BV4596.A25J64   1992▪
248.8'6—dc20   92-8324

Contents

Dedication

To my wife, Connie, who I love very much
and
To Lynn Brookside who, in helping me write this book,
has taught me what service unto the Lord means.

Foreword

There is an awakening happening in America.

Multitudes of people are recognizing that some of the most frustrating problems in their lives and the lives of those whom they love are the result of emotional injury or starvation.

Typically that injury or starvation is the result of physical, emotional, or sexual abuse or neglect that has happened during the earliest years of life.

When I first started hosting a daily radio talk show in Los Angeles more than a decade ago I had no concept of the extent to which people's lives and homes in our culture were being thrashed by abuse. I knew that there were victims of incest and molestation and other kinds of mistreatment, but I viewed them much like people view lepers: I knew they existed and I was in favor of their getting help but I couldn't say I'd ever met one that I knew of.

Several things changed that for me.

One was hosting the radio program. Over a period of ten years I had about seventy thousand conversations with people on the radio, most of whom were hurting deeply, and I welcomed more than seven thousand guests to the microphones to help me and my listeners be better informed. It didn't take long for me to realize that there was something going on in my culture that I had not previously seen or understood. The extent of abuse and other forms of deep emotional injury was bigger than I had known. It was as though the fog had lifted and when I looked over the American and the American Christian landscape, I saw droves of deeply wounded people and understood how much we had learned to hide our pain and to pretend it is not there. I saw human debris and recognized why so many in our country were being attracted to the message of recovery. I also saw in a fresh way how much the church needed to be the place of refuge and healing for a hurting culture and how much the message of Christ applied to what was going on. More significantly for me, I came to realize that abuse had touched my own life and family.

Another factor that helped me understand the significance of emotional injury and starvation was Dr. Mark Johnson.

I was pastoring a church in Long Beach, California, and Mark and his family came to be a part of our congregation. Over a period of time we became friends and I developed a deeper love and respect for him and for the work he was doing as a psychologist. I became impressed with his intelligence, his understanding of hurting people and his commitment to the Lord.

A milestone day in my life was when Mark invited me for breakfast because he wanted to talk with me about a member of my family whom he had met and had the opportunity to talk with at some length. This family member had struggled with tormenting and puzzling personal problems for years and had sought various kinds of help but without relief. Dr. Johnson stunned me by saying, "Rich, I think we're dealing with a victim of abuse here, probably sexual molestation and possibly incest." That insight on Dr. Johnson's part turned out to be shatteringly accurate and that family member was able to embark on a pathway of getting the kind of help that finally answered all the baffling questions and began the season of recovery. Mark was also a significant help to me personally in overcoming the emotional pain that has been in my life.

Mark Johnson is, in my opinion, one of the most valuable voices in the country regarding emotional injury and starvation and brings with him the invaluable perspective of a Christian who has been in the trenches with hurting people. He is willing to consider any and every factor that might contribute to a person's emotional disability: physical, psychological, and spiritual. Additionally, he has done battle with the enemy and learned his tactics and offers a reasonable hope to those who are trying to tiptoe their way through the minefields of abuse.

Rich Buhler
Orange, California

Introduction

He has sent me [Christ] to bind up the brokenhearted, to proclaim freedom for the captives and release from darkness for the prisoners,... to comfort all who mourn, and provide for those who grieve,... to bestow on them a crown of beauty instead of ashes, the oil of gladness instead of mourning, and a garment of praise instead of a spirit of despair. Isaiah 61:1-3

IN THE YEARS SINCE MY OWN REBIRTH into the family of God, my work as a psychologist has brought to me a wide variety of wounded people. Many of their emotional problems are the result of misperceptions regarding themselves, the world around them, and most important, God. My experience has shown that Satan is the real culprit in maintaining these falsehoods, and he will use any means at his disposal to prevent the wounded from really hearing and receiving the truth. I have come to the conclusion that spiritual warfare is a much needed component of any psycho-therapeutic endeavor. It is key to our recognizing Satan's lies and receiving God's truth.

As a result of the abuse or neglect we suffered as children, we have come to believe a multitude of lies. They need to be rooted out and exposed to the light *before* we can effectively counter them with God's truth. Satan knows that he has a much better chance of getting us to believe him if we feel unsure of the truth. And it is difficult, if not impossible, to firmly believe a truth when we have not yet identified the lie that opposes it. Our conviction regarding the truth of God's Word is what will give us the confidence to enter into spiritual warfare on our own behalf and on behalf of those we love.

Often the devil is painted as a being whose whereabouts and tactics will forever remain a mystery. Nothing could be further from the truth. As soldiers, our response to Satan's encroachment on God's territory should include an ability to see Satan's tactics and to understand how God's Word applies to our lives. In addition, we must be able to cry out to God in prayer. That is why I have written this book—to help and encourage those who may have suffered abuse or neglect as children to reclaim the power that comes in knowing that God has claimed us as his very own.

A SURVIVOR'S PARABLE

Perhaps the plight of the survivor can best be understood in the context of a parable—similar to the ones Jesus shared with his followers when he walked the earth. As you read the following story, ask God to use it to enlighten you about your own condition as his child.

A farmer was given a parcel of land by his parents. Unfortunately, the land was never very productive so he was extremely poor. Each time the farmer thought he finally had a chance to get ahead, circumstances like the weather or market prices took a turn for the worse. The farmer felt hopeless. It seemed as though he had spent his entire life just trying to get by.

One day a rich young ruler of a far away kingdom met the farmer. The ruler told him that the land the farmer lived on was actually his. The parcel had always belonged to him and, in fact, he had purchased it at a great price. The rich young ruler invited the farmer to remain on the land and manage it. He taught the farmer the rules of land management and promised that if he observed all the rules, the land would become very productive. In addition, the ruler promised that he would return someday to the farm and take the farmer home to rule with him in his kingdom.

The ruler warned the farmer that there was a thief in the vicinity. The thief's name was *Fear*. He would be unrelenting and would come to steal all that the farmer had. He said that *Fear* would sneak onto his land quietly under the cover of darkness. While the farmer was understandably frightened by this news, the ruler told the farmer that he could protect himself from this thief. The ruler advised the farmer to put up high fences on each side of the land in order to keep *Fear* out.

Each of the four sides of the fence was to be built with a different kind of material. One was to be constructed with *knowledge of the truth*. Another side was to be built out of *conviction*—a heartfelt certainty that everything the ruler had told him was true. Another was to be built out of *boldness* and the willingness to fight back. The last side was to be constructed of *forgiveness* and the willingness to let go of the hardships of the past. The ruler warned that each side of the fence was equally important for the farmer's security, and then he left.

Time passed. Then the farmer realized that some of the supplies he had kept in his barn were missing. Somehow, the thief had gotten through. The farmer went in search of the break he knew must exist in his fence. He found that the portion of the fence composed of *truth* had fallen down. The farmer recognized that he had recently listened to several false rumors and had begun to worry about his relationship

with the ruler. After securing the fence with a proclamation
of truth, the farmer again felt safe.

A little while later, however, the farmer realized that the
thief had gotten through once more. This time he discovered
that the fence made of *conviction* had fallen down. The
farmer now saw how he had proclaimed the truth, but hadn't
really done so from his heart. After all, the ruler had been
gone a long time. The farmer was feeling neglected and
hurt. He quickly wrote a letter to the ruler sharing his concerns and mailed it the next day. Suddenly he felt better,
knowing the ruler would read it and respond with love. Now
the fence of *conviction* was standing once more.

But the thief again stole from the farmer. This time he
found that his fence of *boldness* had fallen down. The farmer
had failed to stand by this fence and openly resist the thief's
intrusions when he sensed his presence. He would have to
get mad and fight back rather than spending his time worrying about whether the ruler would truly return for him.

Finally, the fence called *forgiveness* gave way and the thief
stole once more. The farmer took a moral inventory of his
life and realized that he had failed to forgive his parents for
leaving him so poorly prepared for managing a farm. Once
he had finally forgiven his parents, his fence stood erect and
his land was secure.

Over the years the farmer learned how to fight the "fight
of faith" to protect his land from *Fear*—just as the ruler had
instructed him. He was finally safe and his land productive.
When the ruler returned, he was extremely proud of the
farmer. Placing a crown on his head, he took the farmer
home to live in a castle the ruler had built especially for
him.

As you read this book, I pray that you will grow in your
own knowledge of the truth, the heartfelt conviction of that
truth, and the boldness and willingness to fight against fear
and thus defeat the thief. I also pray that you will develop an

ability to forgive those who have hurt you in the past. Although the thief may seem frightening, he is a cowardly enemy, no match for the spiritual weapons we are given in Christ. Those weapons are based on the truth of God's Word and give us victory over the tactics of the one who wants to steal our faith—Satan. He is the thief we must war against. My sincerest wish is that when the Lord returns for you, he will find you safe and productive, ready to live forever in your heavenly home.

Mark Johnson, Ph.D.
San Clemente, California

ONE

We Wrestle Not with Flesh and Blood

For our struggle is not against flesh and blood, but against the rulers, against the authorities, against the powers of this dark world and against the spiritual forces of evil in the heavenly realms. **Ephesians 6:12**

S OME TIME AGO A COVER OF *Time* magazine caught my eye. The word "EVIL" appeared against a backdrop of total darkness. Under it was the query: "Does it exist or do bad things just happen?" I am convinced that victims of childhood abuse and neglect need the answer to that question more than any other portion of our population.

Are we the victims of happenstance only? Or is our struggle not against "flesh and blood," but rather against "spiritual forces of evil in the heavenly realms"? Coming to grips with this question is essential for those who want to overcome the damaging effects of abuse or neglect.

Both of my parents were alcoholics who battled chronic depression. My father was also a sex addict. His cache of pornography and his endless pursuit of the ultimate sexual experience dominated his life. He dragged my mother off to see the latest X-rated movies on Saturday nights. His desire to spice up their marriage also increased profits for the makers of the provocative lingerie he insisted my mother wear. He made it clear to my mother that sex was all he really needed from her. That fact was a great source of shame for my mother.

My mother was also an alcoholic. In addition, she made my brother and me the focus of her life. Invested in getting us to need her, she saw to it that we lacked nothing. Circumstance seemed to cast my brother in the role of "The Whiz Kid," my mother's emotional confidant. She took pride in the fact that—just like my father—he excelled in everything he did.

As the second-born child, I had a penchant for getting into trouble. Playing the role of "The Loser," I struggled in school and always seemed to need someone to rescue me from my most recent failure. I learned that all I had to do was act helpless and my mother would intervene—usually by asking my brother to bail me out. Meanwhile, my mother's hunger for love produced children with an unhealthy dependence on her.

My parents' addictive style left its mark on us. My brother fought alcoholism and I struggled with drug dependency in my early adulthood. In addition, my father had taught me to carry on his sexual addiction through a fascination with pornography.

After my first marriage failed, I began to read much of the literature intended for adult children of alcoholics. It seemed to have been written just for me. Issues of codependency abounded in my life. I began to explore theories pertaining to dysfunctional families. Information on the "inner child" was also helpful.

I quickly became convinced, however, that psychological theories were simply not enough. My study of dysfunctional families and four and one-half years of therapy did little to alter my constant despair. I directed an appeal toward heaven, challenging God to prove his reality by banishing the darkness that blanketed my soul. As a result of my plea, I experienced a new birth in Christ. But my conversion experience failed to touch my deepest pain.

As a relatively new Christian in 1981, I read Hal Lindsey's *Satan Is Alive and Well on Planet Earth*.[1] It was one of the most engrossing books I had ever read. I found almost every page to be frightening, inspiring, and ultimately encouraging. In the course of reading Lindsey's book, I came to see the true source of human suffering. As a practicing psychotherapist, this timely information challenged all of my educational background pertaining to human personality and the practice of psychology. I was suddenly aware of the reality of a spirit world.

Some years later I read Scott Peck's *People of the Lie*.[2] This book had a similar effect on me. I began to look at evil from a psychiatric point of view. I realized that as I treated clients who had been victimized, I needed to be aware of the degree to which evil was involved in the events of their past.

As I began to apply my newfound understanding of evil to my practice, I also saw my own past in a new light. I discovered that my heart had become numb because of conveniently forgotten, multiple childhood losses. I needed to release the intense grief within my heart. Eventually I learned to acknowledge the childlike part of my spirit. I cried out to God and in the process learned that he was my Abba Father—my "Daddy-God."

I also began to see that I had lived out my life according to numerous vicious cycles which tended to maintain my highly self-defeating behavior. Those cycles were based on several faulty beliefs about the way I was meant to relate to the world. So I set about learning to embrace truths about who I was in the Lord. I learned to live as a "new creation in Christ."

I also realized that there had been a force of evil at work in my family for generations. My grandfather was in his seventies when he put a gun to his head. A great aunt ended her life through an overdose. A great uncle chose asphyxiation as his way out. All through my childhood, I was frightened by the fact that my father seemed to regard suicide as an option if things got to be too much.

My mother also seemed to be headed for the worst. Her physical health seemed tentative and became especially poor whenever things didn't go her way. Her response to a fight with my father was invariably an illness. When my father finally threatened to leave her, my mother contracted cancer. She battled the pain of cancer for years, always suffering devastating flare-ups in response to emotional upheaval in her life.

Sadly, my father eventually joined the ranks of family members who had believed death's promise of lasting peace. While in a drunken stupor, he used a rifle to find release from his private demons. After years of struggling with cancer, my mother decided that life without my dad was too much to endure. She chose to abandon all medical treatment. She died before my eyes as I sang to her, "Jesus loves you, this I know."

As I became increasingly aware of the effect of evil throughout generations of my family, I realized that I couldn't afford to remain ignorant about spiritual warfare. God expected me to be actively engaged in the "fight of faith." That point was brought home to me in many ways.

But God's final lesson in spiritual warfare got my attention because my very life was at stake. One day a dear friend—one of the psychiatric nurses I work with—offered to pray for me. Since we are accustomed to praying for one another, her offer didn't seem unusual. I sat down while she placed her hands on my shoulders and began to pray.

Her words caught my ear instantly. She said she felt that something needed to be stripped off of me. She named it "death." As she continued to pray, I opened my eyes to see her symbolically gesturing—pulling something away from my face and off of my body. She prayed about other things that day as well, but it was the image of her stripping away an invisible presence that sent shivers down my spine.

That same evening my wife asked me about a spot on my skin under my beard. I had never really noticed it. She was so concerned that she called a dermatologist the next day. He determined that I had a deadly form of skin cancer which he said we had caught just in time.

Paul's words came back to me as I remembered my friend's prayer. "We wrestle not against flesh and blood." I believe that a spirit of death had lurked within my family for generations. Its attempt on my life was cut off through a prayer offered in response to the leading of the Holy Spirit. God had, in effect, slipped his glasses on my friend as she prayed for me that day so she could see the thief's presence.

Through this experience, I realized how much could be accomplished in the fight against "spiritual wickedness" when we learn to see things through "God's glasses." With them we can see supernatural events that take place all around us in our journey through the natural realm.

How is it that something as sinister as the specter of death could become so familiar to a household? As a victim of my parents' alcoholism and their not-so-subtle death wish, I was taught to regard death's call as familiar, even comfortable in a strange way. I had been blinded to God's truth in my life. As a result of my brush with death, I recognized my need for a greater knowledge of the principles of spiritual warfare.

I have learned that interaction with the family of God is a major factor in our healing. Another necessary step in our recovery is learning to separate ourselves from the lies we have come to believe as a result of our victimization. Those very falsehoods made it possible for spiritual oppression to overtake us in the first place. And I have seen it demonstrated over and over again that prayer is an essential part of the healing process.

These insights have become the cornerstone of my practice. And I have been privileged to watch as God healed the wounds of scores of people, setting them free forever.

Does evil exist? Or do bad things just happen? Evil does

exist. Its presence is palpable at times—even measurable—and must be countered with spiritual warfare. Our fight of faith will make it possible to lay hold of God's promise that we are "more than conquerors."

My prayer for you is that God will give you his glasses to use as you read this book. I hope that what you see won't frighten you, but rather make you fighting mad and able to see who your real enemy is. It's not God, your parents, or the capriciousness of life. Your real enemy is Satan. And we have already been named the victors.

IF I'M A VICTOR, WHY DON'T I FEEL VICTORIOUS?

From the instant the serpent duped Adam and Eve and all of humankind was spiritually lost, Satan has been trying to prevent us from finding our way back to a position as sons and daughters of God. When we commit our lives to our heavenly Father, through his Son Jesus Christ, Satan's plan has failed. But Satan isn't willing to accept his defeat quietly.

As victims of abuse or neglect, we have been emotionally abandoned by our caretakers. We begin to believe that there is no one there for us and never will be. Our abandonment shapes our lives in ways contrary to God's perfect will. Even when Satan fails in his intent to prevent us from knowing the one true God, he tries to capitalize on our sense of abandonment. If he can get us to spend our time dealing ineffectively with the pain of our emotional wounds, then he can trick us into believing that we continue to be emotionally abandoned despite our spiritual adoption (see Rom 8).

Paul tells us in the sixth chapter of Ephesians that "our struggle is not against flesh and blood, but against the rulers, against the authorities, against the powers of this dark world and against the spiritual forces of evil in the heavenly realms." It would seem that the forces of evil are set against us within a hierarchy all their own.

Satan is identified in Scripture as the god of this world, the accuser of the brethren, the adversary or enemy, a prince of demons, the ruler of the kingdom of the air, the prince of this world, the ruler of darkness, the tempter, and as the evil one. Quite a clear picture of a being who wants nothing less than our destruction. In fact, John 10:10 describes the devil as a thief who comes "only to steal and kill and destroy."

But how does Satan set about attempting to destroy us? We read: "He who does what is sinful is of the devil, because the devil has been sinning from the beginning" (1 Jn 3:8). In other words, he uses men and women like us. Satan uses the sins of our parents and the unintentional mistakes that ooze from their own wounded spirits. He uses circumstances, our youth, our friends—whatever means are at his disposal.

But the good news is still this: Christ came not only so that we might have life as God's children, but so that we might live it abundantly.

LIFE'S THREE BASIC QUESTIONS

When we grow up in a dysfunctional—and consequently toxic—home environment, we sustain profound losses. Survivors of childhood neglect or outright abuse suffer significant debilitation—physical, mental, and spiritual—at the hands of others. In fact, it is essential for the Christian counselor to see the results of victimization not only from a psychological standpoint but a spiritual one.

The damage on a spiritual level is frequently the most difficult to recognize and to deal with because it is below the surface of our minds. This spiritual damage involves an inability to think properly or to feel anything that bears witness to what is hidden in our hearts. Numbing strategies and the lies we have been taught make it impossible to cry out our real pain to God.

As survivors of abuse and neglect, we feel that something precious has been stolen from us, and rightly so. Frequently, we have lost our purity, innocence, wholeness, well-being,

and sense of belonging. Those losses can result in a broken-
ness of will and spirit that is nearly crushing.

Our victimization caused us to come to numerous erroneous conclusions regarding our worth as human beings and
the moral choices available to us. We grew up believing that
we were the exception. Somehow we felt so damaged or
despicable that we alone lacked whatever intangible qualities
make a human being "deserving" of love. We never knew that
we had intrinsic value or that we deserved to be loved simply
by virtue of our existence.

When Satan can use our circumstances to teach us that we
have no worth, we become vulnerable to all the other lies he
wants us to believe. If we have no worth, then our feelings
and perceptions must also be worthless. So if our caretakers'
craziness conveys the attitude that Mommy's reliance on pre-
scription drugs or Daddy's violent temper is "normal," then it
must be true. If they imply by their conduct that it's natural
for Mommy and Daddy to pass out each evening or for
Daddy to touch us in "those places," then who are we to
argue?

When we believe that the painful events of our lives are
"normal," then we also come to believe that the best we can
hope for is safety through capitulation. Sometimes we give in
to those demands in one blinding moment of pain. More
often we capitulate through a lifetime of surrender to the
dull ache caused by the death of our dreams. By giving in to
our abuser's demands—whether verbal or circumstantial—
we hope only to *survive*. All other goals are abandoned in the
hope-crushing atmosphere of our dysfunctional families.

As all children do, we assume that our caretakers are accurate representations of the nature of God. As we accept their
faulty perceptions of us and the world around us, Satan is
happy to use those misperceptions in his effort to keep us
from knowing God. Circumstances often seem to work to
Satan's advantage.

Once we have a personal relationship with God, Satan continues to capitalize on those misperceptions. He knows that as a result of Christ's death and resurrection, he has already lost the war. But, if he can cause us to be consumed with denying our pain, with controlling our environment and relationships, with scrambling to make ourselves feel safe, he can still claim a victory in at least some of the battles of our lives.

A philosopher once said that every human being has within him or her a "God-shaped vacuum." God created us to seek him. He created us with a need to worship him. All of Satan's efforts are devoted to filling our need to worship God with something other than God.

Our need to know and worship God generates two questions every human strives to answer during his or her early, formative years. We are also born with an inherent need to avoid pain, which serves the basic function of self-preservation. This brings into play a third question with which children commonly grapple.

Life's three basic questions are:

1. Who am I?
2. What is my purpose?
3. What must I do to be safe?

For those who grow up in a healthy environment—where our caretakers manifest selfless, godly love—finding the answers to these fundamental questions is a wonderful adventure. These fortunate children learn to believe that the world is safe, because they are encouraged to meet its challenges only to the extent that they are ready. As their caretakers model godly love, they learn that they have intrinsic value, that they are worthy of love. They grow up understanding that they are made in God's image and have the right to become the people God created them to be.

For those of us who grow up in an unhealthy atmosphere, Satan's plan involves providing the wrong answers to these three questions—answers that smear God's name. Our caretakers create circumstances that imply a god who must be angry or displeased with us. Satan uses our abusive homes to teach us about a god whose love must be earned. We come to know a god of expedience, power, and selfishness—a god who lies and manipulates, who uses people.

Our inborn hunger to know God is fed with a poisonous presumption about his character. So the answers to our first two questions—as supplied to us by a hostile environment—are based on information contrary to the Scriptures. They are lies. In fact, Christ was speaking about Satan when he said, "He was a murderer from the beginning, not holding to the truth, for there is no truth in him. When he lies, he speaks his native language, for he is a liar and the father of lies" (Jn 8:44).

Having been given the incorrect answers to our first two questions, the answer to the question about our safety is bound to be tinged by frightening impressions of the world. Fear becomes a constant in our lives. Just as it's true that perfect love casts out fear, so it is also true that constant fear blocks out love. Consequently, our view of life is distorted. We come to see God as someone to be feared, despised, or simply disregarded. Inadvertently, we pass that view on to our children. And so it passes from generation to generation.

The biblical promises are glorious: a heavenly Father who reaches out with loving arms; freedom from condemnation and shame; an abundant life. Yet they seem only to mock us and the faith we claim. We struggle to walk the narrow road with eighty-pound packs on our backs, while those around us seem to glide by. And always the questions add to our burden. "Why? What's wrong with me? Has God failed or have I?"

Neither has failed. There is hope. Hope comes in knowing that the truth sets us free. Consequently, we need to destroy the stronghold Satan has formed in our lives through his distortions of the truth. In order to overcome their influence and to claim a more abundant life, we need to "demolish arguments and every pretension [everything] that sets itself up against the knowledge of God, and we take captive every thought to make it obedient to Christ" (2 Cor 10:5).

That isn't as simple as it sounds. We must learn to differentiate between the inaudible cry of our hearts and the lies our circumstances have taught us. This is difficult because our hearts have grown coldly silent over time. The silence that brought safety and survival killed us emotionally as well. We need to hear our own cry for help once more and learn to express it.

Then we need to embrace the truth: *God is for us.* Satan strives to keep us locked safely in a prison formed of the lies we learned as children. We have developed names like "codependence" and "low self-esteem" for our prisons, but they remain prisons, nonetheless.

When we begin to take steps to recover from the wounds of abuse or neglect or even our parents' innocent mistakes, we are engaging in a spiritual battle. Christ has already purchased our freedom. We have only to use the sword of truth in order to claim it.

Neil Anderson, author of *The Bondage Breaker,* says that we must avoid accepting commonly held yet basically false notions about Satan's hold on us.[3] These falsehoods result from believing that a particular kind of power is required of us to gain our spiritual freedom. It is truth that sets us free from the devil's influence over us. Anderson states: "The power of the Christian is in the truth; the power of Satan is in the lie.... The truth is what makes an encounter with Satan effective." The truth, rather than some personally achieved spiritual power, is what is essential to the success of our warfare.

In order to emerge victorious from our warfare, we need only one weapon—*the Word of God.* Through his Word we learn the nature of the battle we face. We learn about our armor and its effectiveness. We learn that we have an ally in the Holy Spirit. We learn that while demons may compose a formidable enemy, God says: "Do not be afraid or discouraged because of this vast army. For the battle is not yours, but God's" (2 Chr 20:15).

The sword of the Spirit, which is God's Word, is said to be so sharp that it can cut through every lie that may lodge itself in our heart. "For the word of God is living and active. Sharper than any double-edged sword, it penetrates even to dividing soul and spirit, joints and marrow" (Heb 4:12). It really is the only weapon we need.

GOD'S ARMOR

Ephesians 6:13 tells us to put on the full armor of God. We appropriate the *belt of truth* by attaining a general knowledge of God's Word, which is truth. The belt worn by a soldier in the days when Ephesians was written actually held all the rest of the armor in place, keeping it tight against the body. So it is with our armor. The truth of God's Word is what holds all the rest of our armor in place. When we wear the belt of truth, we have an absolute certainty within our own minds that the Word of God is true and reliable so that we can use it with confidence.

The *breastplate of righteousness* is composed of the righteousness of Christ, which we possess by virtue of our adoption into the family of God. But in order to remain sure of our breastplate, we need to act in accordance with the Scriptures. And we must continually avail ourselves of God's forgiveness through confession of our failures and weaknesses. Then we can turn a deaf ear to the accusations Satan is sure to whisper to us.

We are ready to meet any challenge we may face when we wear the *shoes of the gospel of peace.* When we have shoes on our feet, we're ready to go wherever and whenever God might have us go. We do this by running to his Word when we are in trouble or hurting. We can be at peace with God and ourselves knowing that in spirit, we are already seated with him in the heavenlies. Our position is secure. When there is a broken relationship between us and our brothers and sisters in Christ, we can also run to them with the gospel of peace.

The shield was a protective covering soldiers used to deflect the blows of the enemy. Our *shield of faith* is forged from an unswerving perspective—keeping our eyes firmly fixed on Jesus. It is our utter conviction that God's promises are ours as a result of our redemption.

Once we are born again, we already possess *the helmet of salvation.* The helmet is meant to protect the head—the mind—from the attack of the enemy. With the helmet of salvation firmly in place, we can meet the questions Satan may whisper to us regarding the validity of our salvation with the assurance we have in Christ Jesus. We can be secure in the knowledge that *nothing* can separate us from the love of God (see Rom 8:37-39).

And the *sword of the Spirit,* of course, is the Word of God as we *apply* it to our daily lives. An unused sword tends to become rusty. A sword can be used both offensively and defensively. We wield the sword of the Spirit when we speak the Word of God aloud to counter spiritual harassment and temptation.

Each piece of our armor is important. Indeed, the effectiveness of each hinges on the others. Satan raises lies against us, much as an enemy in ancient times raised his own banner over his army. Ultimately, being equipped to do battle with those lies requires that we see ourselves as God sees us. God's banner over us is love (see Sg 2:4). Once God's love becomes real to us, we will suddenly find ourselves willing to let go of our stubbornness, self-sufficiency, and need for control. Trusting ourselves to the plans of one who loves us absolutely is easy.

As survivors, we may struggle with the idea that we must put on the whole armor. For us, the suggestion that we have to *do* something puts us right back into the old mindset. We are immediately back to *performing* rather than *being.* The moment we feel we are expected to perform in some way in order to please God, we find our faith quickly slipping away.

We need to recognize that Christ is already in us. We need only appropriate what is *already* ours. We may find it easier to put on the full armor of God if—rather than visualizing the armor as something that's slipped over our head and shoulders—we visualize it as God's arms enfolding us. What better armor could possibly exist?

I like to envision myself climbing up into my heavenly Father's lap. If we are to be "big" enough to face our adversary, we need to allow ourselves the wonderful comfort of becoming "little" once again. When we admit to our Daddy-God our weaknesses, powerlessness, and sense of vulnerability, we become willing to snuggle down into his loving arms and rely on *his* protection. Seeing ourselves as Christ sees us allows us to set aside our need to be self-sufficient because we see our childlike nature from God's perspective. God has given us an opportunity to have a second childhood—the childhood we always wanted and needed, but were never permitted.

Once we know the power of the weapons we carry, Satan can no longer "push us around." We need to understand the power available to us through our "big brother," Jesus Christ. It is in the name of Jesus that we can take authority over the spiritual realm. "Therefore God exalted him to the highest place and gave him the name that is above every name, that at the name of Jesus every knee should bow, in heaven and on earth and under the earth, and every tongue confess that Jesus Christ is Lord, to the glory of God the Father" (Phil 2:9-11).

When we speak the truth in Jesus' name, we have dominion over even the spiritual forces of wickedness. We can bind their power, break their assignments against us and those of our bloodline, and cause them to retreat, all in the name of our Lord Jesus Christ.

THE SINS OF THE FATHERS

Exodus 20:5 says: "You shall not bow down to them [idols] or worship them; for I, the Lord your God, am a jealous God, punishing the children for the sin of the fathers and fourth generation of those who hate me."

Idolatry and rebelliousness carry stiff penaltie leave a family open to the influence of demons f years to come. Many families have spirits that nave been "passed down" from generation to generation. My own family is a prime example. A spirit of death had gotten its way with generations of my ancestors who viewed suicide as a way out. It was only due to the lessons God taught me about spiritual warfare and my rights as a believer that I was able to rid myself—and future generations—from that curse.

The forces of darkness will gleefully ignore our legal standing as children of God for just as long as we will allow them. What's more, Satan capitalizes on unconfessed sin. When that unconfessed sin involves idolatry (including witchcraft and other occult practices) and rebelliousness, Satan has a legal right to harass our families unto the third and fourth generation. As the forces of darkness continue to harass our children, they fall prey to the same sins that gave Satan his "rights" within our bloodline in the first place. Thus we have a never-ending cycle. That cycle will continue until we confess our ancestors' sins of idolatry and rebelliousness so that they are wiped away by the blood of Jesus.

TELLING THE MOUNTAIN TO MOVE

Fear is a major factor in the lives of those who were abused or neglected as children. God designed the family to protect and nurture little people until they are old enough to be responsible for themselves. When the family falls down on the job—for whatever reason—the children feel powerless and vulnerable. Fear often takes hold.

The feeling of powerlessness we had as children plagues many of us into adulthood. Yet, Jesus told his disciples that with faith the size of a grain of mustard seed, "you can say to this mountain, 'Move from here to there' and it will move.

Nothing will be impossible for you" (Mt 17:20).

Fear is the power source for the forces of darkness. Faith is the power source for the kingdom of God. Job says, "What I feared has come upon me; what I dreaded has happened to me" (Jb 3:25). And 2 Timothy 1:7 says, "God has not given us a spirit of fear, but of power and of love and of a sound mind" (NKJV). Scripture clearly sees fear as a spiritual issue.

In a pamphlet called, *Fear: Breaking the Bondage*, Charles Neiman suggests that fear will "attract demons like blood attracts sharks.... Fear comes out of your heart, goes into the spiritual realm and spreads like a cloud."[4] Demons then capitalize on that cloud of fear.

Of course, Satan and his cohorts don't just capitalize on our fear, they have tricks for inducing it. They use the words others speak to us or they whisper lies to us themselves. They trick us into focusing on the problem rather than the solution, or harass us in order to magnify the problem. And Satan uses any means at his disposal to convince us that we should maintain our silence. He knows that a secret shame provides fertile ground where all kinds of lies can take root. That's one reason why we are told to "... confess your sins to each other and pray for each other so that you may be healed" (Jas 5:16).

If we keep hiding the shame that stems from the trauma we suffered as children, we are left living in darkness. Hidden shame keeps us from entering into God's light and prevents us from gaining the experiential knowledge that "there is now no condemnation for those who are in Christ Jesus" (Rom 8:1). Fear keeps us in bondage and torments us. "There is no fear in love; but perfect love casts out fear, because fear involves torment" (1 Jn 4:18 NKJV).

In that same pamphlet, Charles Neiman says, "Fear feeds on misinformation. Fear feeds on half-truths. Fear feeds, breeds and multiplies on lies."[5] Conversely, the truth sets men free. Jesus said, "Sanctify them by the truth; your word is truth" (Jn 17:17).

THE TRUTH AND NOTHING BUT

Proverbs 29:25 tells us, "Fear of man will prove to be a snare, but whoever trusts in the Lord is kept safe." But how has God provided for our safety?

Being familiar with God's Word sets us free from fear caused by misinformation. Along with that, knowing who we are in Christ offers power and safety. It is my hope that this book will help you in your search for the truth about who you are in Christ. Besides the Scriptures included in this book, look for others that God may cause to come alive to you.

Hebrews 10:14 tells us: "For by one offering [Christ's death] He has perfected forever those who are being sanctified" (NKJV). Once we are born again into the family of God, we are perfect. Only our sanctification has yet to be completely accomplished.

Knowing that we have power with which to fight the forces of darkness through the name of Jesus Christ also provides us with safety. Intimately knowing the one who keeps us safe— our heavenly Father—helps us to feel secure. We can be sure that he is steady and unchangeable. He has all the attributes we long for in our earthly fathers, and God's heart towards us is expressed through our adoption into his family.

When we are well acquainted with God and his qualities, through the study of his Word, we can never be tricked into believing that he will abandon us. When we are confident that he loves us and wants only the best for us, and when we know absolutely that he is sovereign—that he never loses control of the events of our lives—then we can put aside all fear of circumstances. And we can be absolutely convinced "that in all things God works for the good of those who love him..." (Rom 8:28).

"This is the victory that has overcome the world, even our faith" (1 Jn 5:4). And, as we know, faith moves mountains.

A Practical Exercise

✦ ✦ ✦

1. If you believe that generational sin exists within your family, ask God to reveal it to you. God isn't in the business of keeping secrets from us. He will gladly breathe the truth into your mind and heart through his Holy Spirit. Ask God to give you a divinely inspired impression of what sins your ancestors may have committed that need to be confessed.

2. Once you have that information, confess those sins on behalf of your family and ask forgiveness, claiming the blood of Jesus. Confess any sin of your own that remains unconfessed also. Then separate yourself and future generations—naming those descendants whose names you know—from the sins of your ancestors in the authority of Jesus' name. Here is an example of a prayer like the one you might need to pray:

   Lord, I confess the sins of idolatry and witchcraft that my ancestors practiced [substitute or add whatever other sins God may have revealed to you]. I forsake and separate myself, my children, their children, and all future generations from those sins. In the authority of Jesus' name, I cover those sins with the blood of Jesus and I declare that all curses resulting from them are null and void.

3. Once you have prayed, it would be wise to command aloud any familial spirits to depart from you and from your household in the name of the Lord Jesus Christ.

TWO

A Call to Battle

I pray also that the eyes of your heart may be enlightened in order that you may know the hope to which he has called you, the riches of his glorious inheritance. **Ephesians 1:18**

R UTH HAD ALWAYS BEEN her stepfather's favorite. Despite his abusive battering of every other member of her family, she was very proud of the fact that she alone had managed to be "good enough" to avoid his wrath.

But Ruth was distressed by the fact that she hadn't been able to achieve the same perfection in the rest of her life. In fact, she described the rest of her life as a shambles. At the age of thirty-three, Ruth was still unable to point to one thing in her life that she had ever finished. She always seemed to quit just short of success.

She had enjoyed a very promising start as a singer, but cut her career short just as she was beginning to acquire a small degree of celebrity status. Ruth had no explanation for her decision to give up singing. She simply decided to quit one day and that was that. Though she was certainly intelligent enough to have finished easily, she even quit high school.

When Ruth first sought my help, she had recently become a Christian. Although she had been promiscuous earlier in her life, she was now trying hard to practice sexual abstinence. But even though she tried to "be good," Ruth admitted that she frequently engaged in sexual behaviors with her current boyfriend. She was ashamed and suffered terrible guilt—frequently followed by bouts of depression. She just couldn't seem to "control herself."

Ruth was upset by the fact that every man she had ever known seemed to be an enigma. The way she spoke about men indicated that she feared them as much as she worshiped them. She had come to the distressful conclusion that she would never enjoy true intimacy. She believed that her stepfather's favoritism was probably the closest thing she would ever know to love.

Some time after Ruth began seeing me, she reported having a very vivid dream. She dreamed that an assailant forced her to the ground and made her look at the head of a snake as he held it within inches of her genitals. It was apparent to me that Ruth's unconscious had supplied a clue to her past. Her mind had served her well by repressing any memory of abuse in order to protect her from the truth about her relationship with her stepfather.

This struggling young woman still maintained that he had truly loved her and had treated her better than he had treated anyone else in the family. Yet Ruth's behavior—and now even her dreams—clearly pointed to the fact that she had been victimized. I explained to Ruth that homes where abuse occurs are nearly always closed systems in which every member is targeted for some type of abuse. I asked her to ponder the question, "How did I escape my stepfather's physical battering?"

During one of her subsequent sessions, I asked Ruth to draw a family portrait as a therapeutic exercise. When she had finished the drawing, I noticed that she had drawn her stepfather with his back towards the rest of the family. Only the back half of his frame was in view. I asked, "What do you suppose the front of his body looks like?" I suggested that Ruth pray, asking God to reveal the truth to her, and then to draw another picture.

The next day—while Ruth was aimlessly doodling—she was surprised to find that she had drawn a chillingly explicit picture. In the drawing was a man facing a little girl with his genitals exposed.

Then Ruth broke her long silence. She finally saw clearly that all the "love" she had received from her stepfather was only a different form of abuse from what her siblings had received. She had been her stepfather's favorite at a horrible cost.

Now Ruth was able to come to grips with the reason behind her continued failures to practice sexual abstinence. Her stepfather had covertly communicated to her that sex and love were inextricably bound together. As all child victims do, she had desperately grasped any shred of evidence that she was loved. Shame and humiliation were all she ever actually received from her father. She seemed to exhibit a need to return to those familiar feelings frequently.

Ruth had a secret. In an effort to draw attention to the secret, her unconscious perpetuated the cycle of sex, shame, and guilt. And the only way to break the cycle was to break her silence. You see, the power of evil grows in the dark. Silence is simply another form of darkness. Ruth's silence kept her trapped in a vicious cycle.

In order for her to break that cycle, Ruth had to begin to give voice to the cry of her heart. It was terribly difficult for her to break her lifelong silence. But knowing that the powers of darkness triumphed in her silence provided her with the motivation to keep trying. After some months of therapy, we began to tap into the strong emotions within her and she began to acknowledge the true depth of her pain.

FINDING ROOT CAUSES

Victimization touches all of us. Every one of us has either survived victimization or knows intimately someone who has. For the casual reader, the word "victim" may simply mean someone who "got ripped off." To the counselor, the term may mean that someone bigger, more powerful, or more shrewd has violated the will of another. For those of us who were misused in this way, the word "victim" produces whispered echoes of words like "wimp," "loser," "crybaby," or "loner." At a deeper level, the word may resonate with feelings of self-hatred, learned helplessness, self-deception, and ongoing despair.

In actuality, a *victim* is anyone who has been physically, sexually, emotionally, or spiritually exploited through either overt or covert aggression or control. Physical or emotional abandonment constitute victimization as well. Many professionals suggest that the trauma of abuse leads to psychological, emotional, and social difficulties of all kinds.

A leading psychiatrist is of the opinion that child abuse is the cause of a major portion of the mental health problems in the United States today. He describes survivors as ticking time bombs who suffer from pervasive emotional difficulties. In the case of incest, for instance, survivors commonly suffer from marital difficulties, ongoing physical problems, conflict with extended family members, and self-destructive behavior.

Many people remember all too clearly the hurtful experiences of their childhood, but some victims found they could not cope with the pain so they tried to forget the abuse ever happened. Children may force themselves to forget in order to protect their fragile sense of personal security. But family memories are buried at the expense of a sense of personal history. In order to perpetuate the illusion of safety, we forfeit the right humans have to see our past as part of a whole. In Ruth's case, such repression of memories had devastating effects.

These repressed memories can show up later in a lot of problems that seem to have no root. While the licensed professional may be equipped to identify the child victim, the adult victimized as a child may go unnoticed and untreated. In today's eager quest for the quick fix, clients often enter therapy looking for a way to get "all better" in twenty weeks. They want the external behaviors dealt with so that they can "get on with life."

The exploration of deeper therapeutic issues may be scrapped because superficial issues are more quickly identified and dealt with by the therapist. Clients and insurance companies often encourage therapists to choose a more superficial treatment path because treating symptoms rather than the root cause appears to take less time and money. Treating only symptoms rather than dealing with a root cause, however, allows clients to continue hiding from the true source of their pain.

More important, what is hidden gives Satan one more advantage. What is held in secret allows him to silently condemn us. We will eventually come to think that he knows about our past better than we do. Our "secrets" bring a sense of foreboding and shame that keep his lies believable. Eugene O'Neil wrote: "None of us can help the things life has done to us. They're done before we realize it, and once they're done, they make us do other things until, at last, everything comes between us and what we would like to be, and we have lost our true selves forever."[1]

It's true that none of us can help the things that happened to us as children. *But we can make choices to recover in the present.* There seems to be only one way to regain "our true selves." We must open the closet door of our memories and face what we may have hidden from ourselves. We must uncover our past—with all the pain and trauma it carries—before we can be healed. Only then will Satan be defeated. God's light will reveal Satan's accusations for what they truly are.

CLUES FROM THE HEART

There is a purpose to all our behavior. When we interpret these clues correctly, they can help us to become aware of our unresolved pain and will often reveal the cause of that pain. The statements below provide a sort of blueprint of the survivor's thought patterns and can provide a glimpse into his or her inner world.

A thermometer measures a symptom, thus signifying that something may be wrong with the body. In just the same way, the thought patterns represented in The Victim's Creed can provide an emotional thermometer that may expose an "ailment" of the heart. The cause of that ailment, while hidden from view, may be a past that is too frightening to look at or too painful to remember.

The Victim's Creed

1. Pleasure must be stolen and thus, can never be enjoyed.
2. If I have to wait for something it won't happen.
3. If I work as hard as I can I will just pass. There's no hope for an "A."
4. No matter how hard I work, some part of me says, "You could have tried harder."
5. No one could possibly be happy with me the way I am. Therefore, I must change.
6. No matter how hard I try, nothing will ever change.
7. I always feel guilty about something.
8. I feel safest when no one pays attention to me.
9. I hate myself whenever anyone shows disappointment in me.
10. People only look out for themselves. Consequently I can't trust anyone.
11. I am powerless, insignificant, and can't stand up to people.
12. Whatever I'm doing right now, I know there's something else more important I should be doing.
13. Rewards are to be earned. It's just that I've never been quite good enough to deserve any.
14. Whenever I've decided to reward myself, I've taken too

much or delighted myself in the wrong things, such as food, sex, booze, etc.

15. When someone tells me no or says "You can't," I get really angry and refuse to listen anymore and often go ahead and do it anyway.

16. My mind is always racing. I'm always thinking and wondering why I behave the way I do. There's something really wrong with me.

17. I hate my body.

18. I hate myself.

19. I don't think anybody will ever understand and besides, I don't know how to tell them.

20. I know God keeps score.

21. I feel like God is getting fed up with me. I've blown it too many times.

22. If the truth were known about me everyone would see what a phony I am.

23. If I just try harder, Lord, I know I'll get it right next time—I promise!

24. If I start blowing it again, God will wait for me to finally learn my lesson before he'll come and rescue me.

25. I keep sinning and I don't think I can stop. Maybe I don't really care or maybe I'm just beyond help.

When a survivor of abuse is born again in Christ Jesus, these erroneous conclusions don't just disappear. If we fail to deal with the reason we originally came to these conclusions, many of us find ourselves unable to overcome them. This may cause us to wonder about the validity of our conversion. We may ask, "If conversion and spiritual regeneration are God's gifts to everyone who believes, why do I continue to act and feel the way I do?"

Unfortunately, the answer we frequently receive—when we even have the courage to ask the awful question aloud—is that we lack faith and need to spend more time in God's Word and in prayer. While I agree that the study of Scripture and prayer are essential to recovery, survivors of abuse often need more.

GOD IS OUR REFUGE

The Victim's Creed indicates a thought life riddled with doubt, self-blame, excruciating guilt over almost everything, along with a perfectionistic streak that's nearly paralyzing. As victims, we are robbed of the joy and satisfaction found in accomplishing life's simplest tasks. We are victims of the tyranny of our own thought life. And Satan loves it. We are so busy telling ourselves the lies born of our instinct to survive that he can just sit back and enjoy the tragedy as it unfolds.

Our thought lives are infected with reproach. We are annoyed at our feeling of vulnerability... but vulnerability to what? Our feeling of being at risk to further harm emanates from an unconscious level. It eludes our reasoning and our efforts to identify it. Our self-talk is condemning and hopeless. We're quietly telling ourselves: "I'm powerless. I can't protect myself."

We also have an underlying belief that we are alone, that nobody cares. This belief ultimately produces feelings of isolation and a nebulous, ever-present threat of abandonment. When we were children, forgetting meant survival. Now it may serve only to keep us from perceiving the truth that can set us free.

As O'Neil so eloquently stated, survivors often feel that they have lost themselves. That sense of loss prevents them from living the kind of life they yearn to live. As Christians, our dilemma is even greater. Just as Ruth was, we are often caught in a cycle of prayer and repentance. We aspire to be all God intends us to be, yet perceive the goal as unreachable.

Our emotional losses have effectively handicapped our relational skills. Our ability to offer or receive love has been damaged. We may feel genuinely incapable of loving ourselves or others. Christ admonished us to love the Lord with all our heart, soul, and mind (see Mt 22:37). For many of us, this commandment only fuels our self-condemnation because of our inability to love.

But the God we serve is a faithful God. He wants to teach us how precious we are to him. He wants us to understand fully that he is our Abba Father—our Daddy-God (see Rom 8:15). Dare to believe that "The eternal God is your refuge, and underneath are the everlasting arms" (Dt 33:27).

A Practical Exercise
✦ ✦ ✦

If you believe that you have embraced some of Satan's lies as a result of abuse you endured as a child, the following steps may prove helpful. You may want to take these steps whenever you begin to feel doubtful that God's promise of healing is for you personally.

1. Read and memorize Jeremiah 29:11-14: "'For I know the plans I have for you,' declares the LORD, 'plans to prosper you and not to harm you, plans to give you hope and a future. Then you will call upon me and come and pray to me, and I will listen to you. You will seek me and find me when you seek me with all your heart. I will be found by you,' declares the LORD, 'and will bring you back from captivity.'"

2. Remind yourself daily that God is in control of every event in your life. Nothing escapes God's notice and no situation ever just "gets away from" him. Accept your present circumstance for now and live in hope for your future. But give yourself permission to feel and express your feelings to God through prayer.

3. Pray the following prayer or something like it in your own words:

I rebuke you, Satan, in the name of the Lord Jesus Christ. I resist fear and declare that any spirits causing me to fear must go where Jesus Christ commands them to go, never to return.

Lord, I stand before you in need of your healing touch. You see my heart, Lord, and are well acquainted with my needs. I ask, in the name of your Son, Jesus Christ, that you banish all fear from my life, and that you set the healing process into motion in my heart and mind. Amen.

THREE

Telling Secrets

"Don't be afraid," the prophet answered. "Those who are with us are more than those who are with them." **2 Kings 6:16**

TRISH WAS A SICKLY TEENAGER who was having difficulties in school when her mother brought her to me for counseling. The girl's major physical complaints were pre-ulcerative colitis and severe migraines. She had been examined repeatedly by her family physician and a host of medical experts. None of them could make a definitive diagnosis and many indicated that her problems were primarily psychological.

Trish's parents had divorced when she was eleven years old. After four years, she was still fighting the despair and hopelessness apparently resulting from the divorce. Because her father spent much of his time away from home even prior to the divorce, Trish had perceived him as "distant." Just before her parents had split up, her mother had become a Christian, taking the children to church on Sundays. Her father had chosen not to join his family in church and had moved out of their home shortly thereafter.

Trish had languished. She had gone to church with her mother and sister each Sunday but didn't see her relationship with God as anything more than a secondhand experience. Attending worship services had seemed to be merely a way to pass the time on Sunday mornings.

Despite my attempts to help Trish grieve over her father's departure, she gained little relief from her symptoms. I came to the conclusion that her pain couldn't be attributed solely to his loss. I suspected that the teenager's agitation over her parents' divorce disguised a much deeper source of pain.

One afternoon I received a frantic phone call from Trish's mother. Her daughter had been sent home from school that day because her legs had quit working–she couldn't walk or stand up. The onset of this paralysis had been sudden and dramatic. Her mother rushed her to yet another specialist. The doctor was unable to find any cause for Trish's loss of the use of her legs. She and her mother returned home dejectedly, where—miraculously and spontaneously—her paralysis left her and her strength returned. I asked her mother to bring Trish to my office the following afternoon.

Once the three of us were seated in my office, I explained that Trish's problem was likely of psychological origin and explained a condition called hysterical paralysis. I added that the mind is capable of creating symptoms in our body which are a manifestation of an inner conflict. For example, soldiers in combat sometimes lose the use of their arms or legs due to hysterical paralysis following a firefight. The burden of having killed another human being can prompt a soldier to seek relief from his guilt through an unconscious process that leads to paralysis.

I suggested to Trish and her mother that the girl's temporary paralysis was most likely symbolic. Perhaps there was something in her past she didn't want to remember but couldn't run away from—something which nevertheless continued to haunt her. Trish was astounded by the idea that the mind was capable of making memories inaccessible on a conscious level.

Not by coincidence, that same evening Trish began to remember an event from her past that had lain hidden in the recesses of her mind. Her family's lively discussion about where to go on their upcoming summer vacation tapped her unconscious memories. Trish began to have disturbing flash-backs of an event that had occurred four years previously.

While lying on my office couch the next day, the images of that life-changing experience began to flood back to her. Trish's story unfolded over the next few sessions. The picture returning to her indicated that she was traumatized while on a vacation with her family when she was eleven. She had ventured off to the family's cabin to get a towel, while the rest of the family waited for her at the lake.

Along the way Trish saw a man grab a woman and pull her into one of the cabins. Through the door that was still ajar, Trish watched horrified as the man raped the woman and then hit her repeatedly with his fist until she lay unconscious. She stood there in total shock, unable to take her eyes off the scene.

Even though Trish had escaped unnoticed, the violence had horrified her and impressed upon her a need for silence. The trauma was so great that the young girl's mind had cooperated by blocking out every vestige of the event. While her trip back to the lake took longer than her family had expected, they had been engrossed in the fun of swimming. Trish returned without her towel, yet never indicated to her family what had happened. She had repressed her memory of the ordeal within minutes.

GETTING AWAY FROM IT ALL

A survivor of childhood trauma once said, "The longer I tried to ignore my abuse and the bitterness I held in my heart, the more I fell apart. Why? Because what I buried, I buried alive!"

Hiding from the truth—whatever our reasons—simply doesn't work. Yet there may be many reasons for a survivor to hide from the truth about what he or she has endured. As in Trish's case, we may fear further harm or retribution. We are afraid of being blamed.

We may fear that harm—emotional or otherwise—may come to someone we love and whom we desire to protect. We believe it is kinder and more loving to shield them from the truth. We often feel it is necessary to remain loyal to the victimizer who may occupy a role as protector and authority over us. We also fear the disruption of the family system which represents stability, however meager.

Fear becomes a primary motivating factor in our lives. We feel guilt and shame because of the abuse and try to escape those feelings by distancing ourselves from what has happened to us. We numb our hearts to the pain... and to most other emotions as well. Frequently, fear becomes the only emotion we can truly feel.

Fear works to Satan's advantage. It convinces us that what is hidden must be kept out of sight. The longer such traumas are repressed, the scarier they become. We know that things "in the night" can get us. Fear tells us simply to hide under the covers. Our hearts oblige and the numbing process begins.

When we are victimized, we choose—on an unconscious level—to appropriate a distancing strategy called *denial*. This denial of reality takes place when reality is too frightening for us and we find it "safer" to alter it. Denial seems essential to our survival, but actually serves to perpetuate our fear. The fear simply goes underground where it won't be openly acknowledged and dealt with. So when we carry our denial into adulthood, it serves only to keep us trapped within walls formed of fear, repression, and shame.

In Trish's case, her sudden hysterical paralysis provided the clue to her past. For others the symptoms are often less dramatic but equally eloquent.

A SURVIVOR'S DISGUISE

Kevin had been seeing me for several months in an effort to process the painful emotions resulting from childhood abuse. Even after dealing with the shame of growing up in an alcoholic family, his behavior remained symptomatic. He related to the world in a way that indicated an inner pain untouched by all that he had accomplished in therapy. Additional trauma seemed likely.

Kevin continued to demonstrate agoraphobic tendencies —a generalized fear of people and places—and continued to engage in compulsive rituals involving hand washing and cleanliness in general. His behavior indicated an unconscious need to banish the nagging fear that he was dirty inside.

But what made him feel dirty? Keeping in mind that all behavior is purposeful and that compulsions are aimed at reducing an unconscious fear, we began to look more closely at his symptomatic behavior.

As therapy progressed Kevin related to me that his hand-washing rituals had begun in the fourth grade. Eventually, he began to remember disconnected bits and pieces of a trip to the zoo with his Boy Scout troop. Kevin was inadvertently separated from the group. He recalled few specifics but did remember standing in front of a mirror in a public restroom washing his hands repeatedly—unwilling to leave the sanctuary of the washroom.

When Kevin returned home he hid in the garage, very much afraid. The reason behind that fear, however, was still not within reach of his conscious mind. Weeks of intense therapy followed, during which time he gave himself permission to acknowledge the pain and grief of a nightmarish event he could finally recall. With time and diligence, the pieces fell into place.

Bit by bit, Kevin put together a picture of a little boy who happened to witness a man masturbating behind some trees. In his frantic attempt to make a quick getaway, Kevin had slipped. As he landed on the ground, he got mud all over his hands while the man shouted profanities at him. Confused and badly shaken, the boy found his way to the safety of a public restroom. Once he had washed his hands, he could forget the event—but his unconscious continued to allude to it each time he returned to a sink and a bar of soap.

Eventually Kevin remembered that the man had grabbed him as he ran away, screaming that he would "come after him" if he ever told anyone what he had seen. Kevin's mind had taken the ultimate, protective stance. He couldn't tell what he couldn't remember. Now he could see that he wasn't crazy, as he had feared. He had simply been stating the truth in disguise.

Kevin's fear of further harm had produced a need to hide the truth. Repressive processes were put into motion. Because maintaining the secret seemed to be of paramount importance, the secret itself became something to be feared. The boy was absolutely certain that the stranger would return to avenge himself if he ever told anyone. The door to his unconscious opened to receive his secret, then quickly closed again.

But Kevin's feelings of overwhelming fear, guilt, and shame couldn't be so neatly sealed away. As he attempted to relieve himself of those feelings, their control over his life increased. His secret had to be exposed to the light before healing could occur.

OPEN OUR EYES, LORD

As childhood victims of abuse or neglect, we may have embraced a sort of psychic blindness in order to protect ourselves. Unfortunately, now that we are adult survivors, we continue in our blindness, and this blindness intensifies our fears. Satan keeps us from seeing the help at hand. The Old Testament prophet, Elisha, and his servant once found themselves in a predicament that is somewhat similar to the one in which we may find ourselves.

When the servant of the man of God [Elisha] got up and went out early the next morning, an army with horses and chariots had surrounded the city. "Oh my lord, what shall we do?" the servant asked.

"Don't be afraid," the prophet answered. "Those who are with us are more than those who are with them."

And Elisha prayed, "O LORD, open his eyes so he may see." Then the LORD opened the servant's eyes, and he looked and saw the hills full of horses and chariots of fire all around Elisha. 2 Kgs 6:15-17

Those of us who have been wounded by childhood victimization may feel a lot like Elisha's servant. We see only what our circumstances and our past permit us to see. A deep-seated belief is operating in our unconscious, telling us that "there is no one out there" to support us in our pain. We look up and see only our symptoms and fears surrounding us, bearing down on us like the army that surrounded Elisha. We feel hopelessly isolated.

But God can slip his spiritual glasses over our eyes, just as he did with Elisha's servant. God calls on us to view things with an open, trusting heart. Elisha chose to look to God rather than to be afraid. We need to learn to see the invisible army of God ready to defend us. We have to become willing to look over the walls of our defenses, beyond our symptoms, to the relief that is at hand.

Second Timothy 1:7 says: "God has not given us a spirit of fear, but of power and of love and of a sound mind" (NKJV). Fear is a spiritual condition. Bearing our pain in silence—and the shame that often goes with it—only serves to multiply our fear. We need to invite God into the process. He can teach us to walk by faith, not by sight (see 2 Cor 5:7). He will supply us with the faith we need as we hear his Word (see Rom 10:17).

God is able to see us through the frightening process of learning to trust him—even when we feel as if we must close our eyes, hold our breath, and leap off a precipice in order to demonstrate our faith. We must learn to rise above the numbness inside of us and cry out our pain, fear, and shame to him.

THE LIES WE BELIEVE

Correctly interpreted, our behavior supplies us with information that can help us identify the lies we have come to believe. Once we have identified the falsehoods we have embraced as the result of our abuse, we can combat them with God's truth. Then the Father's love can penetrate our fear as his comfort overcomes our pain.

Understanding the language of victimization is extremely helpful enabling us to interpret what has happened to us as children. Just as the Victim's Creed indicates the nature of the inner world or thought life of the survivor, our overt behavior can indicate a crippled ability to relate to the world outside ourselves. The following is a list of common signs and symptoms of those who have been victimized.

Emotional signs of victimization. Survivors often suffer from chronic and long-term depression and free-floating anxiety. Emotional aloofness, mistrust, and a tendency toward social isolation are also common. They are plagued by generalized fears of being trapped, embarrassed, or caught off guard.

Victims of abuse may demonstrate a frenetic style of relating to the challenges of life, exemplified by the need to do things "right away, right now, hurry, hurry, but... where do I begin?!" They are also subject to compulsive behaviors of all kinds, and may exhibit extremes in eating, drinking, or sexual behavior.

Survivors frequently show a tremendous need to control situations, other people, and their own expressions of emotion. They frequently manifest performance anxiety because of a feeling that everyone is evaluating them. Consequently, their performance must be perfect. As we saw earlier in the Victim's Creed, survivors are often highly critical of themselves and others and become extremely depressed, frustrated, and angry when met with failure.

They tend to be "rescuers," believing that everyone else needs to be fixed. They frequently choose a helping profession like nursing or teaching for their life's work. Or, they choose a profession that allows them to avoid most human contact and gives them a sense of control over their circumstances and the outcome of their efforts. Computer and library sciences are common choices, though certainly only a small portion of the people who choose to work in those fields may be survivors of abuse.

Finally, guilt and shame characterize their thinking about almost everything. Their guilt is an expression of their underlying belief that whatever has or will go wrong is their fault. A former client of mine said he carried around "enough guilt to fill the Grand Canyon." Don felt guilty about everything and was always apologizing to me for things he thought he had done wrong. Whenever I was late to his appointment, he would apologize for inconveniencing me since I was obviously so busy. He even apologized for not being a better client. Don assumed that he should be showing more feelings, gaining more insights, and making more progress. He was convinced that he never performed well enough.

The survivor's emotional symptoms suggest that he or she was trapped and made to perform in some way—through physical coercion or threats, spoken and unspoken. He or she learns to place a heavy emphasis on performance because love is always something to "earn."

As children they were paralyzed with fear, guilt, shame, doubt, confusion, and despair. Ultimately, they try to bring some sense of order into their world by becoming compulsive, emotionally constricted, or constantly combative. As children they comforted themselves by adopting "magical thoughts." If something was wished for, longed for, or worried about long enough, they believed it would either happen or be avoided altogether, depending on their wish.

Physical signs of victimization. The physical ailments of survivors are numerous. "Somatization" often comes into play. We "somatize" when our psychic pain becomes physical. This unconscious process assigns the task of keeping the secret to various organ systems or muscle groups. In other words, the body is made to reflect, through symbolism, the nature of the trauma in order to continue defending the secret.

For instance, a fixation on the mouth or its related musculature often develops as a result of sexual trauma to that part of the body. Survivors of oral rape will often find it difficult to open their mouths widely without fear. And they often grind their teeth, developing Temporal Mandibular Joint pain (referred to as TMJ), and other similar complications.

Survivors frequently suffer from muscular tension, particularly in the neck, jaw, and shoulders. They tire easily. They often develop chronic headaches because of tension around the eyes that results from holding back tears, or because of the underlying terror stemming from having seen too much.

Gastrointestinal difficulties and problems with constipation or recurring diarrhea are common. Female survivors frequently report being constantly plagued by PMS-related symptoms. Sexual dysfunctions of all kinds are common to both sexes.

"Body memories" often emerge as therapy progresses. That is, survivors often reexperience the physical sensations they felt during the original trauma. These physical sensations are recollections of the trauma to which the child was subjected that are stored in the brain at a level where no reasoning takes place. These body sensations often provide a disturbingly vivid representation of what happened to the adult as a child. In cases where the survivor experiences body memories, the body itself is doing the talking. This sort of memory—when it can be identified—can be particularly helpful in cases where trauma took place during the preverbal stage of their development.

Ritual behaviors. Ritualistic signs are those behaviors in which the survivor repeatedly—almost hypnotically—engages. The behavior takes on a magical appeal. Examples might include making certain that everything is in its place before going to bed at night, sleeping with a light on, repeatedly checking the locks on all the doors and windows throughout the evening, and so forth.

Survivors may focus on a certain part of their body with extreme concern regarding its appearance or function. For instance, they may give their mouths supercilious attention by repeatedly brushing their teeth. They may feel a need to chew on something, or to avoid anything uncomfortable or foreign on the lips or near the mouth. And, as in Kevin's case, the hands often receive similar attention. Compulsive handwashing and the spreading of lotions are not uncommon.

Obsessions with cleanliness are frequent. Survivors may become extremely uncomfortable when exposed to dirt, strong odors, or various kinds of physical touch or closeness with others. Embracing may be terribly difficult, as well as any other sense of physical intrusion. Being touched may remind them of something they don't want to remember.

"Compensatory behavior" is a psychological term that refers to a survivor's need to compensate for a traumatic event by replacing unpleasant sensations or emotions with those having a more desirable effect. This sort of behavior may develop around the body part originally involved in trauma because of the shame felt in regard to that portion of the body. It can consist of things like cleaning, attending to, or endlessly fretting about the affected body part.

Rituals involving bodily elimination may also come into play. Survivors may dress or undress laboriously while maintaining certain observances such as removing underwear only while looking away from the mirror or only in the dark. Certain parts of the body may never be exposed or touched. Their attire may reflect the need to hide much or all of their body.

Sometimes survivors observe counting rituals or exhibit tapping movements or rocking movements in particularly stressful situations. Fetishes of all kinds are fairly common. The child victim may adhere to a conviction that thinking in a certain way or doing things in a particular order will magically produce desired results. For instance, one young lady would never uncross her legs or remove her purse from her lap while in conversation with me. Another client always insisted I leave the office first at the conclusion of our sessions together.

The child visited in the night by an unwanted intruder may develop extreme concern over sleep patterns. Perhaps a child sleeps on her tummy and, coincidentally, an intruder doesn't disturb her that night. She may conclude that her sleeping position afforded her a measure of protection. Or a child may believe there is magic in refusing to look into the mirror prior to going to bed, or any number of other normally inconsequential acts. In other words, they frequently assign a magical quality to an insignificant factor.

As child victims, they grasp a forlorn hope by claiming what safety can be found in magic. And although the safety is only imaginary, they are lured by desperation into repeating the behaviors they have assigned magical properties. So they adhere to rituals born out of happenstance in their desperate desire to feel safe. The vulnerability of childhood makes magical thought and wish fulfillment alluring. Ritualistic behaviors that remain in force into adulthood are simply regressive attempts at self-preservation.

Signs of victimization in fantasies and dreams. Survivors are often terrorized by their dreams: being chased and caught by unknown assailants; being abandoned or left behind; being punished or ridiculed for doing something wrong; being murdered, robbed, beaten, or molested. Dreams in which a baby is lost or neglected in some way are common. Dreams about spiders are often reported as well. These bizarre dreams are extremely frightening, with the stories sometimes taking on perverse overtones.

One of my clients repeatedly dreamed about being watched while in a public restroom. Later in the same dream, he would find himself being forced to undress and submit to various perverse sexual acts. Our random thoughts and even our daydreams can leave us distraught and feeling guilty or ashamed of what they must imply about us.

One young woman felt a compelling need to touch the genital areas of the various dolls lying about in her child's room. Though she never succumbed to the impulse, it shocked her and caused her to worry that she was in danger of becoming a child molester. She feared that her need to touch the dolls' genitals would be transferred to human victims. A male client was plagued by obsessive thoughts about touching other men's genitals while in public restrooms or on the street.

The survivor's previous childish need to magically undo things through dream work or wish fulfillment play themselves out in their adult imaginations. Their dreams and fantasies become a means by which they attempt to rewrite a traumatic event or somehow make the event less threatening through familiarization. Since the unconscious keeps the secret frozen in time by the very act of repression, the need to undo the traumatic act remains just as strong as it was when it first occurred.

The survivor's need to gain some sense of power and control over his or her feelings of vulnerability and victimization can take on an overwhelming importance within that person's thought life. Actually, survivors are merely trying to find a way to desensitize themselves to the unconscious fears they have held in check for so many years. Because the original conflict has not been resolved, fear never abates and becomes the cause of ritual behavior.

Survivors often suffer an inability to enter into a healthy sexual relationship. They are frequently promiscuous, or find themselves in destructive relationships involving infidelity, homosexuality, sadomasochism, battering, betrayal, etc.

Survivors' lives are often a paradox. They can frequently look back on years of loose living, in which sex was the primary focus of almost every relationship. After marriage, however, they may discover that they feel trapped by the bonds of wedlock and begin to avoid sex altogether or put up with sex, secretly begrudging it.

While their physical symptoms may be most easily observed, survivors' hearts, souls, and minds are affected too. Their minds are plagued by the falsehoods they have embraced regarding their relationship to the world and what that indicates about their moral and social acceptability. Their hearts are affected by their erroneous conviction that strategies such as denial and repression will successfully distance them from their pain. Their souls are damaged because surrender to God becomes a frightening reminder of times when they were asked or forced to give too much of themselves.

If you believe that you may be a survivor of childhood abuse or neglect, but have no memories that would cause you to be sure, you might do well *not* to make an assumption in that regard. Find a good therapist (the afterword in this book may be of assistance) and ask for his or her help in determining whether or not you are a survivor.

If you *are* a survivor, take heart. Nothing is beyond God's ability to heal and rectify.

A Practical Exercise

✦ ✦ ✦

1. State aloud this affirmation of faith: "God has given me all the power I need to overcome my past because Christ died, shedding his blood for me. In the name of the Lord Jesus Christ, I claim that power right now. I declare that I no longer need to use the tricks I learned as a child for overcoming feelings of powerlessness and vulnerability."

2. Ask God to bring it to your conscious attention whenever you engage in compensating techniques and compulsive behaviors. When those behaviors become apparent, list

them all and release them along with any shame you experience into God's hands. Claim his healing power over each in Jesus' name.

3. Pray a prayer of opposition to the forces of darkness that may have come into your life as a result of childhood abuse. The prayer below is simply a model which you may wish to adapt to your own needs and circumstances.

Satan, you have been rendered powerless by virtue of Christ's death and resurrection. All power and authority over you and your demons has been given to me in the name of the Lord Jesus Christ. I declare, by the power in that name, that all of your efforts to keep me from knowing the truth must cease right now.

Further, I declare that you, Satan, have no right or power to prevent me from knowing the truth about my past and the ways in which you may have used the abuse I endured as a child to cause me to come to erroneous conclusions about my place in the world and my standing in God's family.

Lord, I ask you in the name of your Son, Jesus Christ, to sanctify my mind. Give me eyes that see and ears that hear the truth of your Word and the truth about my past and my present. Amen.

FOUR

The Nature of
Our Warfare

Therefore God exalted him to the highest place and gave him the name that is above every name, that at the name of Jesus every knee should bow, in heaven and on earth and under the earth, and every tongue confess that Jesus Christ is Lord, to the glory of God the Father. **Philippians 2:9-11**

R ECOVERY REQUIRES OUR recognition of the intent behind our abuse. Our abusers are merely pawns in a much larger game. The spirit behind our abuse is the real issue. In *People of the Lie*, Dr. Scott Peck says, "The time is right, I believe, for psychiatry to recognize a distinct new type of personality disorder to encompass those I have named evil."[1]

Dr. Peck describes an "evil" person as having a consistent, destructive tendency toward scapegoating. Such an individual also has an excessive—although usually covert—intolerance to criticism and other forms of injury to their ego. A pronounced concern with maintaining a public image of respectability contributes to a stability of lifestyle, but also to pretentiousness and denial of hateful feelings or vengeful motives. He or she also has an intellectual deviousness, with an increased likelihood of a psychiatric disturbance.

61

In other words, some psychiatric and behavioral disorders can best be explained in the context of evil. In Dr. Peck's profile of the evil individual, one particular feature stands out: *deceitfulness*. The Bible describes a deceitful person as someone who hears the truth, but doesn't do what it says— like someone who, after looking at himself in a mirror, "goes away and immediately forgets what he looks like" (Jas 1:23-24). In psychological terms, such a person is the ultimate rationalizer.

HOW DOES OUR ABUSER'S DECEIT AFFECT US?

When we have been victimized as children, our thought lives become riddled with rationalizations and self-serving delusions—most of them learned from our abuser. A survivor's thought life can be viewed as self-deceptive. We believe that the love we hunger for is available only when we are willing to sacrifice ourselves and endure the pain.

Love and pain, in fact, often become equated in our minds. We convince ourselves that our suffering is not in vain. We never notice that we are being set up by the god of this world. The falsehoods that color our lives place us at his mercy. The true nature of our God-given character is hidden behind our own condemning self-talk. We are then placed in the position of inadvertently aligning our thoughts with the powers of darkness.

MANY VOICES

When Vicky first arrived in my office she was in deep despair. She felt that her life had never made any sense. During her first session with me she recounted a history of drug abuse and promiscuity that started in adolescence and continued until she was well into her adult years. Vicky had recently ended a five-year engagement because she could no longer tolerate her boyfriend's extreme physical and emotional abuse.

In the course of her therapy, Vicky recounted that she had been sexually abused during most of her childhood by her brother and his friends. But, despite her awareness of these events and her continued successful efforts to express her previously suppressed emotions, she seemed to be no better off. She continued to hide in her house, too fearful to go out. Her mind raced incessantly and uncontrollably. At times she entered a dissociative state when she would disconnect from the world around her and go "blank inside"—blankly staring at an object in the room.

Vicky's self-talk consisted of condemning, beguiling, and frightening thoughts that confused her and made her feel worthless and out of control. It became apparent that we needed to identify the lies these "voices" in her head were telling her.

It was possible these voices emanated from her own conscience which continued to condemn her, because as a child she had felt responsible for her abuse. It was also possible that these voices were a reflection of Satan's desire to cause Vicky to feel condemned and helpless, despite her salvation. The voices Vicky heard suggested the presence of "secondary personalities." I needed to more fully understand the attributes of these "secondary personalities" in order to determine the likelihood of demonic involvement as opposed to a purely psychiatric disturbance.

Dr. Peck, as well as many others, suspects demonic involvement whenever a known "secondary personality" manifests itself in the life of an individual—especially when there is also marked confusion and an unusual resistance to treatment. It is necessary to differentiate resistance born of demonic influences from that which is a result of Multiple Personality Disorder (MPD), which I will discuss in chapter eleven. Even when a patient genuinely has MPD, however, demonic involvement may account for a part of the patient's disorder.

We fall prey to darkness and Satan when we unconsciously subscribe to the lies our victimization has caused us to believe. I suspected that each of the lies Vicky believed had "propped a door open" in her mind. The forces of evil were then free to reinforce the original lie as often as necessary.

Because the voices were disguised as her own self-talk, Vicky had learned to agree with them before she was even conscious of them. Our first step was to help her become conscious of their input. I suggested that Vicky repeat into a tape recorder the statements of these various voices. When she had completed that task, I asked her to give each voice a name, describe its characteristics, and try to identify the lies it told her.

Vicky was able to analyze and categorize these voices, thereby separating herself from them. By virtue of this fact, I concluded that we were dealing with demonic oppression rather than a multiple personality disorder. Vicky named eight different voices.

Lila. Lila was characterized as a prostitute. Throughout her childhood, Vicky's brothers and their friends had paid her to keep silent about their sexual liaison. Vicky had merely wanted someone's love. She was willing to accept hurtful substitutes rather than believe no one loved her. But she had come to the conclusion that she had to be bought because her brothers and their friends paid her for returning their "love." Vicky admitted to me that whenever she was alone on the beach, this voice would tell her to offer herself at any price to the next man that came along. She had resisted the impulse, but those thoughts frightened her and served to further convince her that she was no better than a prostitute.

Josie. Josie was an actress. Vicky learned at an early age that her mother had wanted nothing to do with a child that wasn't "cheerful and bright." When Vicky was able to harden herself to her pain and masquerade as a cheerful child, her mother would tell family friends that she was "a sweet little girl." So the voice Vicky named "Josie" continually told her that she mustn't let anyone know who she really was or what she was really like, because she would surely be rejected. She must wear a hundred faces—all of them pleasant—in order to earn the love she so desperately wanted.

Blanch. Blanch was characterized as a murderer. The anger and bitterness that had invaded Vicky's childlike spirit during her years of abuse gave Blanch her voice. Vicky's hatred of men was surpassed only by her fear of them. As a powerless child, she had been repeatedly forced to succumb to men's sexual advances. She had wished for a magic vengeful power and had built her fantasy life on her desire to exterminate men. Vicky had become convinced that the only way to keep from being abused again was to become more powerful and more hateful than those she hated. She confessed to keeping a loaded gun in her home and carrying a switchblade in her purse.

Patricia. The voice Vicky named "Patricia" was a part of her dissociative tendency. As a child, Vicky had come to the conclusion that there was safety in being unnoticed. She thought that if she could remain "invisible," her abusers might not notice her. In addition, Vicky had learned as a youngster that she could simply "go away" when someone was molesting her. She would imagine herself to be a spot on the wall or a figure in a painting or photograph that lay in the scope of her vision as she was violated.

Eventually, Vicky's need to remain invisible caused her to avoid looking at herself in mirrors. If she could avoid looking into her own eyes, she might be spared from seeing the sense of guilt and shame reflected therein. As she grew older, Vicky adopted the habit of wearing dark glasses whenever possible.

Patricia's voice continually reminded Vicky that she must avoid meeting anyone's gaze. The look of another might expose all the evil she felt she embodied. Surely others would condemn her in the same way she condemned herself. The voice had even convinced her that such a look of condemnation might annihilate her.

Kathleen. As the result of the severe abuse she endured, Vicky had come to believe that her situation was hopeless, with only one way out. So the voice she named "Kathleen" continued to whisper in her ear that death was the only real choice she had. Death had become a mysteriously beguiling friend. Vicky had come to believe that only death could deliver her from the horror of her existence into the arms of "real peace."

Vicky's death wish seemed to manifest itself most often in her aberrant eating habits. She frequently practiced bulimic behavior—binging and purging in a dangerous cycle that threatened her life. At other times she would consume large numbers of candy bars, keeping her blood-sugar levels dangerously high.

Elspeth. Because Vicky's childhood had a nightmarish quality, she grew up believing that she would never be safe. "Elspeth" continued to tell her she was in constant danger. Everything was to be feared. This voice succeeded in convincing Vicky that she needed to remain housebound in order to be safe.

Anna. "Anna" was the voice of Vicky's guilt. Since she grew up believing that she was the cause of all of her abuse, guilt became a major factor in Vicky's life. Anna continually whispered in her ear that she was evil and that she needed to rid the world of the evil she represented. This compounded Vicky's death wish.

Susan. "Susan" kept telling Vicky she was helpless and powerless, keeping her in a victim's role with her former fiancé and others in her life. It may seem impossible for a person to claim power greater than her perpetrators—as demonstrated by the presence of Blanch's voice—while continuing to think of herself as a victim. But it frequently happens and is part of the "craziness" that victims sometimes feel. They feel both powerful and helpless—sometimes in rapid succession.

RELEASE FROM BONDAGE

These eight voices persisted in corroborating the lies Vicky had originally believed. The content of their messages indicated the presence of a powerfully destructive influence in her life. She could see how her attempt to protect herself as a child through mental trickery or self-deception had brought her into fellowship with forces of evil. The god of this world was continually telling Vicky that she was deficient, her situation hopeless, and her trespasses unredeemable.

Further, these voices told her that her only hope for survival was to remain in hiding, secretly wishing for magic to rescue her. Each lie provided a "stronghold" or hiding place for a malevolent spirit. In order for Vicky to be set free, we needed to "demolish" those strongholds (see 2 Cor 10:3-6). Once Vicky could see the destructiveness of these lies and their attendant spirits, she was anxious to renounce the lies and expel them from her life, binding their power over her in Jesus' name (see Mt 16:19). Then she was free to begin the process of replacing each lie with the truth.

I warned Vicky that her retorts to these lies were going to have to involve more than an intellectual dissent. They were intended to destroy her. It was essential that she combat them with a heartfelt declaration of her innocence. In order to make it possible for her to do that, Vicky needed to renounce any benefit she had gained from complicity with these untruths.

Fantasizing about murdering her abusers had comforted her; Vicky needed to confess that and ask God to forgive her. She had gained the illusion of safety from dissociating during the times she was being violated; she needed to renounce that benefit also and ask God for healing. I asked Vicky to determine what benefit she had derived from each of the other falsehoods, renouncing it and repenting of each one separately. Then I instructed her to refute each lie with statements of truth from Scripture.

In Vicky's case, her transformation was immediately apparent. Her countenance changed and she was able to cry spontaneously for the first time since she had begun to see me. We used these three steps to obtain Vicky's release from bondage.

1. *Define* the lie's content and identify the spirit responsible for maintaining the lie.
2. *Separate* oneself from the spirit's influence by repenting of one's complicity with the lie and binding its power in Jesus' name.
3. *Refute* the lie with statements of truth from the Scriptures, exchanging truth for the lie (see Eph 4:25).

When we separate ourselves from the lie, we make it possible for God to fill our "God-shaped vacuum" with himself. In completing these three steps, Vicky made a conscious decision regarding whom she would serve. She decided to place her trust in God, not an easy decision for her. Those of us who were victimized as children find trusting anyone to be frightening. For us, the decision to trust God in this way can be tantamount to leaping off a cliff. But, taking these steps made it possible for God to "bring to light what is hidden in darkness..." (1 Cor 4:5).

In psychological terms, Vicky stepped out of denial. She was finally able to throw off her burden of guilt and shame and access her righteous anger and grief without interference. Vicky had a great deal of work still ahead of her, but her recovery process had finally begun.

The lies Satan grafts onto our souls are a reflection of his primary motive. He wants us to believe that love is only available to us to the same degree that we are willing to surrender our own identity. He wants us to close our eyes to our need to live as one who was created in God's image.

By waging war against us through our own thoughts, Satan is able to convince us that we must remain in hiding behind walls composed of his lies. He teaches us that our survival depends on our ability to grasp whatever false hope "magic" seems to offer, rather than on the sufficiency of God's grace.

The apostle James told us: "Resist the devil, and he will flee" (Jas 4:7). Vicky did just that when she decided to hate Satan's lies rather than herself. I have seen many believers come face to face with similar spirits of darkness and dispossess them by standing against the lie that has afforded them a foothold in their lives.

Our enemy, the devil, operates in our lives in the same way the money changers did in the outer courts of the temple in Palestine. The glory and Spirit of God were revealed in the Holiest of Holies within the temple. *We* are the temple of the Holy Spirit in this age (see 1 Cor 3:16; 6:19). The uncircumcised and unrighteous mingled in the outer courts, creating "noise pollution" similar to that in the mind of the victim. The voices of the "money changers" in our minds busily extract payment from us—God's people—as we attempt to make our lives an offering to him.

Jesus' wrath over the presence of those money changers so long ago remains the same today. He is angry on our behalf. God invited Vicky to rise up in righteous indignation, and in the power of Jesus' name to drive away the "money changers" within her "outer courts" so that she could worship the sovereign God within the temple of her heart.

HOW COULD SUCH A THING HAPPEN?

Floyd McClung, Jr., writes in his book, *The Father Heart of God:* "I believe God has designed us to begin our lives as babies totally dependent and vulnerable, because he intended the family to be the setting in which his love is modeled, so the children would grow up feeling understood, loved and accepted. Nurtured in this kind of loving, secure environment, youngsters could develop healthy, God-based self-esteem, and see themselves as wanted, important, valuable and good."[2]

Mr. McClung offers the opinion that those who have suffered hurt and rejection from their families are hampered in knowing God. They are prevented from enjoying real intimacy with him. And a lack of intimacy with the true God creates an overwhelming relational hunger and a need for intimacy with another god.

Our families introduce us to darkness—not deliberately or maliciously, perhaps, but effectively nonetheless. Usually, our caretakers introduce us to the same lies they learned as a result of their own victimization. And, typically, those untruths are continually underscored by evil spirits who have "hung around" our families for generations. Those lies—and the spirits who use them to gain access to us—become so much a part of our family's belief system that they become comfortable and go unnoticed.

A Practical Exercise
✦ ✦ ✦

1. Make a list of any voices you listen to and write out characteristics of each. What do they say about how to achieve safety, love, etc.?

2. Pray to the Lord the following prayer:

Heavenly Father, please show me how Satan has infiltrated my thinking. Show me his strongholds in my mind. Give me the courage to stand against his presence and genuinely get mad at what he has done to hurt me. Amen.

FIVE

Things Familiar

B ILL WAS PROPELLED INTO TREATMENT when his wife stated one night that he was verbally abusive. Bill knew that his anger sometimes got the best of him, but he was very proud of the fact that he got angry only when provoked. He felt that his emotional outbursts should be excused on that basis.

In response to my questions, Bill admitted that winning arguments with his wife—or anyone else for that matter—was essential to him. He saw every conflict, no matter how insignificant, as a matter of life and death. His self-concept hinged on his ability to vanquish anyone who dared to disagree with him. Bill was clearly an angry man.

Over a period of weeks, Bill told me many stories about the fights his parents had when he was a child. They fought over everything. The tension that followed these fights affected the entire family. Bill's father had been a very passive man who retreated from his wife's tirades. Sometimes he would indicate through his facial expressions that he wanted Bill to intervene on his behalf. Bill felt "stuck in the middle."

Bill's mother was out of control much of the time. When she wasn't making caustic remarks or fighting with his father, she was crying because his father was "so unfair." Because his parents seemed to seek his input regarding their constant bickering, Bill came to see himself as "The Whiz Kid." He felt that his worth depended on his having all the answers.

Although Bill saw his mother as having "all the power" because of her overt anger, I helped him to see that his father was an extremely angry individual as well. He had simply chosen to vent his anger in more passive ways that drove his wife "nuts."

Eventually, Bill began to understand that a spirit of anger had become familiar to him by virtue of his parents' behavior. They had given Bill and his sister a distorted view of a marital relationship and "love" in general, while remaining committed to a dreadful marriage completely devoid of respect for one another.

It hardly seems accidental that anger quickly became an integral part of Bill's relationships with women. A number of short-lived romances ended with his dates telling him he was selfish and always needed to have his way. One woman told him that his temper scared her. At the time, he had written it off as "her problem" and eventually went on to marry.

Bill had also incorporated this spirit of anger into the way he related to the world. It was a part of the fabric of his life, nothing new or out of the ordinary. So Bill was shocked when his wife told him that she perceived him as verbally abusive.

Some of us may proudly claim that we "never get angry," so anger certainly can't be one of our problems. But, if we can't get angry or if we can't express it in a healthy manner, then its spirit controls our destiny also. In avoiding anger at all costs, it becomes a false god, something we fear. Whether we bend to its dictates through a front of passivity or through acts of aggression, anger can become our master.

We need to identify the lies we have come to believe as a result of family dysfunction. Those faulty perceptions are part of Satan's attempt to dupe us into believing that our family's way of relating to the world is the only "right" one. Or, at least, it is the only one we know and our heart bends to its dictates. The untruths that become familiar to us as children bring us into direct contact with darkness. Familiar spirits—spirits that have often been with our family for generations—gain access to us.

LIES BORN OF LONELINESS

Another avenue of intrusion for familiar spirits is loneliness. When we grow up in an unhealthy family, we come to believe that we are all alone. We feel there is no one with whom we can discuss our feelings or perceptions. Satan and his demons take full advantage of that feeling. They tell us lies about our circumstances, our judgments, and possible solutions to our plight.

Like Vicky, who could think of no way other than murder to find release from constant sexual violation, we listen to voices that give us equally bizarre solutions to our problems. Or we desperately grasp at any straw that seems to afford us a measure of safety, like a client named Melissa who had claimed an allegiance with a spirit of infirmity when she was a child. Being "sick" kept her safely out of reach of her neighbor, who missed no opportunity to molest her.

MELISSA'S STORY

Melissa had been crying in her room one morning, trying to think of a way to avoid her neighbor's sexual advances. Suddenly it occurred to her that since her neighbor's only excuse for seeing her was to provide transportation home from school, she could avoid him altogether if she was too sick to go to school. So, Melissa played sick that day and many other days after that. Her plan worked. This, in turn, served to validate the effectiveness of the lie she was embracing: "If I'm sick, I'm safe."

Melissa's story suggests that familiar spirits are invited in by apparently random thoughts and ideas that seem to be solely our own. Nothing could be further from the truth. Liars who remain invisible in the shadows of our mind are only too ready to offer their thoughts and ideas about what we must do to cope with our circumstances. Their twisted distortions of the truth are meant to entrap and enthrall us. A warped way of relating to the world soon begins to form the walls of the prison which holds us captive. We must learn how to discern their presence and tell any and every liar where to go.

We can begin to judge correctly the nature of things familiar to us by clearly discerning or recognizing the *character* of the lies we regularly hear. The character of any untruth represents the spirit behind its operation. Here, the focus is on *being*—what likeness we begin to conform to in following the dictates of this spirit.

We must also be able to determine the *content* of what this lying spirit is saying to us. The content can be recognized by reflecting on how we behave in the world—what we do to be safe, loved, etc. Here, the focus is on *doing*.

For example, Melissa's attempt to escape the molestation of her neighbor caused her to fall prey to a lie. Lying on her bed that morning brought the idea that feigning sickness would provide her with safety. By staying in bed and telling her mother she wasn't feeling up to going to school that day, Melissa could successfully avoid having to be picked up by her neighbor.

The thought that offered hope was this: being sick meant being safe. The *content* of the lie required her to feign illness in order to escape. The *character* of the lie was such that being sickly was her only way of guaranteeing her survival. In telling Melissa how she should behave in order to survive, this particular falsehood came to parent this young girl. It became a source of nurture and comfort to her. Consequently, Melissa began to take on the falsehood's likeness as a sickly individual.

I believe that the lie's character was housed in the spirit realm by a real presence. In this case, a spirit of infirmity was present to guide Melissa in her thoughts and actions toward some specific conclusions.

Melissa's lie and the spirit behind its operation manifested itself in various ways. It introduced thoughts about starvation or the need to lie down any time she became fearful. It ultimately drove her toward thoughts of suicide. Melissa began to see herself as weak, incapable, and sickly—someone who deserved to die. After all, she had given in to her neighbor, hadn't she? Melissa began to "walk" in agreement with the lie and to take on its character or spirit.

SATAN, I DON'T WANT YOU ANYMORE!

Being in the company of a lie—as well as a liar—is ultimately destructive to us. We begin to believe the untruth and its many implications about us. Seeing the *content* of the falsehood in terms of our own behavior, as well as the *character* we began to identify with, is crucial for our recovery.

Melissa learned how to stand up against this particular misperception in the context of a group therapy session. Once the lie was clearly identified and its content understood, she was able to see that a spirit of infirmity was behind its operation. As a statement of faith, Melissa was instructed in how to stand up against the spirit by refuting its presence. She did so by speaking truth against the presence of the lie through God's Word, declaring openly that her safety came by way of God's promises to her.

The group quoted Scriptures to Melissa as they coached her to take a stand against the enemy. Scripture became her offensive weapon—the living stone by which a giant was going to be defeated. Verses applicable in a situation like this are many. One only needs to go to the Word in order to find out what God has to say about our strength and safety in him.

For instance, in Psalms we read: "The LORD is my strength and my shield" (Ps 28:7) and "The LORD gives strength to his people" (Ps 29:11). We also read that the Lord will "make me dwell in safety" (Ps 4:8). The New Testament tells us that "anyone born of God does not continue to sin; the one who was born of God keeps him safe, and the evil one cannot harm him" (1 Jn 5:18). Paul tells us that "The LORD will rescue me from every evil attack and will bring me safely to his heavenly kingdom" (2 Tm 4:18).

Melissa was instructed to speak out God's Word as a way of refuting what the falsehood implied about life and her safety in the world. The spirit behind the lie was refuted the moment she realized that she was safe, because her heavenly Father loved her and was making good on his promises.

Melissa was told that not only was speaking that truth important, but getting mad at the spirit was equally essential. Her heart had to decide to whom it would choose to belong. She had to be willing to express her outrage over what her neighbor had done, and how it had forced her into becoming a liar as a way of protecting herself.

This spirit had beguiled Melissa so long ago into thinking that it offered safety through something actually meant for her destruction. It had to be recognized for what it was. She had a right to be mad, and she did not let the opportunity pass her by. Melissa began to scream out loud in a newfound spirit of boldness the scriptural truths she now knew. In doing so, she took issue with what had happened and began to see the innocence of the little victimized girl within. While pounding on a table to show her rage and screaming out her anguish, Melissa told the spirit she was no longer willing to serve it. And she meant it!

It was essential for Melissa to realize that she had the ability to get angry and break out of the silence of her own pain. Learned helplessness and futility could be replaced by a newfound ability to confront any lies she saw in her life. She could choose to stand upon truth instead.

Finally, as a last step toward freedom, I asked Melissa to name the spirit in question, and in Jesus' name to bind its power over her while casting it down. This last step allowed her to see her newfound authority in Christ's name by which she could stand against any liar and render it powerless. The more Melissa realized that she did not have to be sick any longer in order to be safe, the greater her sense of freedom became, and the louder she got. By the time she was done, Melissa had had a good spiritual workout and the enemy had suffered a setback.

Members of the therapy group applauded and cheered. Everyone realized that another little David had won the day against the giant.

AARON'S REBELLION

Israel's first high priest, Aaron, allowed a spirit of rebellion to settle comfortably in his family when he cast an idol in the shape of a calf for the children of Israel (see Ex 32). Aaron's sons, Nadab and Abihu, fell prey to the deceit of that same spirit many years later. They "took their censers, put fire in them and added incense; and they offered unauthorized fire before the LORD, contrary to his command. So fire came out from the presence of the LORD and consumed them, and they died before the LORD" (Lv 10:1-2).

Their familiarity with the spirit of rebellion or disobedience cost Aaron's sons their lives. The familiarity of the spirits who may operate within our families allow abuse and deceit to be reenacted generation after generation. Those spirits will remain with us until we drive them out of our lives like Jesus Christ drove away the money changers in the outer courts of the temple.

Satan's master strategy is always deceit, from the Garden of Eden until the present time. When we believe a lie, we believe Satan. We become his unwitting accomplice in his efforts to kill, steal, and destroy.

Mark Bubeck, in *The Adversary*, points out that lying is a "peculiarly satanic temptation to sin, against God and man."[3] If Satan is able to get us to believe his lies or to begin to lie to ourselves, he has accomplished his task. According to Mr. Bubeck, such an act is akin to inviting a thief to come and live with us, so that he may continue to rob and hurt us. Demons are quite willing to respond to such an "invitation." Believing a lie is not a benign activity but rather one critically dangerous to our emotional and spiritual well-being.[4]

The three steps listed earlier are an integral part of the deliverance all victims need from Satan's lies. These untruths permeate our lives and are evidenced by our poisonous self-talk. Once we are crucified with Christ and raised again to new life, God no longer condemns us. "Once you were alienated from God and were enemies in your minds because of your evil behavior. But now he has reconciled you by Christ's physical body through death to present you holy in his sight, without blemish and free from accusation..." (Col 1:21-22). Why should we stand for self-condemnation? Whose voice are we listening to?

FAMILIAR SPIRITS WHO COME TO STAY

We may need to battle numerous spirits in our lives as survivors of abuse and neglect. While we should not become carried away with the idea of demons wreaking havoc in our lives, it is wise to be aware that they exist, and that as survivors, we may need to do battle with some of them. The following list may help you to recognize some of the more common spirits that seem to take advantage of victimization.

1. Fear or mistrust.
2. Anger or malice.
3. Murder or destruction.
4. Death, morbidity, or suicide.
5. Division or strife.
6. Infirmity or sickness.
7. Control, aggression, or passivity.
8. Lust or pornography.
9. Greed or power.

10. Idolatry or rebellion.
11. Perversion or macabre.
12. Religiosity or false worship.
13. Blame or criticism.
14. Entrapment or seduction.
15. Silence or mutism.
16. Jealousy or entitlement.
17. Mockery or sarcasm.
18. Confusion or double-mindedness.
19. Pride or perfectionism.
20. Self-control or self-denial.
21. Unforgiveness or bitterness.
22. Grief, sorrow, or depression.

A Practical Exercise
✦ ✦ ✦

1. Ask God to show you whether any of these spirits or others are at work in your life. In what ways are the lies you believed as a result of your childhood abuse an informal invitation?

2. Use the three-step process in order to battle whatever spirits God shows you are at work in your life.

   a. *Define* the lie's content and identify the spirit responsible for maintaining the lie.

   b. *Separate* yourself from the spirit's influence by repenting of your complicity and binding its power in Jesus' name.

   c. *Refute* the lie with statements of truth from the Scriptures (Eph 4:25).

3. Resolve to make the following prayer a part of your daily prayer routine.

Satan, I command you to leave my presence, along with all of your demons, in the name of the Lord Jesus Christ. I claim the power of the blood of Jesus which he shed for me. I bring that blood between me and all the forces of darkness. Amen.

SIX

Your Script

For we are God's workmanship, created in Christ Jesus to do good works, which God prepared in advance for us to do. **Ephesians 2:10**

E LAINE HAD DIFFICULTY getting along with people in a natural give-and-take relationship. She spent a great deal of her time trying to get people to attend to her needs and felt easily slighted when anyone failed to recognize her many charming qualities. Men could never please her. After four failed marriages, she wondered whether any man ever would.

The emptiness in Elaine's life finally drove her to seek counseling, but not until she had already spent more than thirty-five thousand dollars on plastic and reconstructive surgery. She had her nose made smaller, her breasts made larger, and had rushed back to the plastic surgeon when a few facial lines caused her to feel old. Despite all these physical "improvements," she continued to feel very unhappy.

Elaine remembered her childhood as "idyllic." An only child whose parents doted on her, she was the center of their lives until she was ten. Then one morning, without warning, Elaine awakened to discover her father preparing to move out of their home. The young girl was unable to make sense of this sudden turn of events. Everything had seemed so perfect. It became apparent in the course of Elaine's therapy

81

that she continued to carry a tremendous load of guilt as the result of her parents' divorce. As a child she had concluded that she simply hadn't been cute enough or good enough to make her parents happy.

Elaine found it extremely difficult to admit to herself that her parents' actions toward her as a child had been motivated by their own dysfunction and selfishness. I could see that therapy was going to be a painful process for her. She finally admitted that many years after their separation, she had learned that her parents had been unfaithful to one another. Little by little, Elaine painted a picture of herself as a pawn in their efforts to emotionally distance themselves from one another. She eventually realized that their constant gifts and attention had flowed from her parents' need to deny their own pain and loneliness.

Elaine's need to develop boundaries was rarely acknowledged when she was a child. Her mother had frequently invited her to sleep between her parents—ostensibly to "keep Mommy warm." Her father pulled her into his lap each evening—showering her with hugs and kisses and calling her "Daddy's little lover"—while her mother sat in the corner looking forlorn. Elaine began to see that although there had been no inappropriate physical contact, she was nevertheless a survivor of emotional incest. This young child had been expected to meet her parents' needs for closeness and intimacy, in a way just as inappropriate as sexual contact of a physical nature would have been.

Elaine began to grieve the loss of an appropriate childhood relationship with her parents. Eventually she recognized that she had been taught to base her life on a lie that had caused her pervasive feeling of emptiness. By using the Christian's Script that appears at the end of this chapter, she learned to allow God to fill that emptiness by redefining her life.

I encouraged Elaine to memorize some Bible verses to use as weapons when the old lies returned to haunt her, with Ephesians 2:10 as a good place to start. In that way, I hoped she would begin to leave behind her inner conviction that she needed to be physically perfect in order to be a worthwhile person. As Elaine learned to use various Scriptures to answer her condemning self-talk, her manner of relating to God, herself, and others changed. She finally knew beyond any doubt that God was not only her spiritual Father, but her loving "Daddy."

A DISTORTED WORLDVIEW

When we are victimized as children, we begin to base our thought-life on a view of the world that is distorted by abuse or dysfunction. The ways in which humans establish intimacy and obtain love become particularly distorted. We embrace numerous falsehoods in response to our caretaker's self-serving demands. We learn—willy-nilly—that love and security can only be obtained through self-deception and the sacrifice of our self-worth and dignity.

As innocent children, we trust those who are in authority over us, never dreaming that they are teaching us to base our lives on a lie. We must be who they tell us we are if we are to gain their love and approval. We embrace the lie in an act of self-preservation. Eventually our life takes on a self-perpetuating distortion of its own as we embrace our assigned role.

Long after we are adults, that assigned role continues to determine how we relate to those around us. The role often reads like a script. Since our "prescribed lines" provide us with a means of dealing with the uncertainties of the play we call "life," we unconsciously incorporate them into our relationships. We hope that as long as we adhere to our script, we will always know just where we stand. Our position may be a dreadful one, but at least it's ours. To a child who lives in an uncertain and threatening world, even that meager measure of security offers some comfort.

Authors who write about dysfunctional families have labeled these roles in many different ways. I have chosen to label them as *The Prince/Princess, The Whiz Kid, The Coward, The Loser, The Deviant,* and *The Eunuch/Matron.* While a child will often take on aspects of more than one of these roles— or may even change roles as the family system changes—one is generally predominant at any given time. Since they actually share many common elements, some of them may seem to overlap. The following descriptions are meant only to give you a general idea of the way in which your childhood home-life may have helped to "script" your present life.

The Prince/Princess. The Prince or Princess grows up believing that he or she is someone's favorite. The abuser often praises the child's beauty, charm, intellect, or other natural asset. These children come to believe that they deserve special treatment.

Elaine's story is a good example of a child who is assigned the role of the Princess. The price for being Mommy's and Daddy's special girl was high. Yet because the emotional incest was carried on within the protection afforded by the lie that such treatment made Elaine special, its price tag remained hidden until she was well into her forties.

Playing the role of the Prince/Princess allows the child to gain some sense of significance and worth in an otherwise hostile world. Often—particularly in the case of physical intimacy—teaching the child to accept such a role whittles away his or her natural resistance to abuse. The abusive act is placed in a favorable—or at least acceptable—light because it makes them "special." The result is that such children are "set up" to become the prey of numerous abusers throughout their lives.

The Whiz Kid. The Whiz Kid is considered to be bright, strong, capable, and perhaps adult-like. By casting children in this role, abusers absolve themselves—at least in their own minds—of the responsibility for caring for them. They convince themselves that the child can handle whatever is asked of him or her. The Whiz Kid is often treated by a parent as a friend and emotional support or caregiver.

In the case of a client named Ray, both of his parents expressed great personal satisfaction with his academic achievements and his "popularity." They treated him as if he were especially gifted—a miniature adult. In fact, his father often visited his bedroom at night so that he could "talk things over with him." At the same time Ray's mother treated him as a friend. She confided all her secrets in her son and complained about her unhappy marriage and her husband's aloofness. Ray grew up to be—in his own words—"the caretaker of the world."

The emotional support required by the adult abuser may include sex, but this element is not necessary in order to be damaging to the child. Whiz Kids come to believe that they are only acceptable to others when they are willing and able to perform the roles of confidant, counselor, and/or sexual partner as needed.

The Coward. The Coward is taught from his or her earliest memory that "everything" makes him or her afraid. "Don't be a chicken!" and "Don't be such a crybaby!" become familiar refrains. The Coward's script teaches the victim that he or she can't stand up to the rigors of "real" life and must accept whatever comes his or her way.

The outcome of such a script is predictable. This child will probably become the family scapegoat or "fall guy" who learns never to complain or fight back. Such a child becomes easy prey for multiple abusers who regard the Coward's mindset as an open invitation to aggressively act out physically, sexually, or—at the very least—verbally.

Jennifer's father was a malicious drunk who often verbally beat her up. He called her names and endlessly criticized her, mocking her hurt expressions and tears. He justified his cruelty with the lie that he was "doing it for her own good," so she would learn to stand up for herself in a hard world. He excused his abuse with his assertion that he "couldn't let her grow up to be a wimp."

The Loser. Losers are convinced that they are a failure or a nuisance and often operate under the conviction that they just don't belong. Such children may discover that they were conceived "accidentally." They may be the "runt" of the household or they may have come along "too late" in their parents' lives. The Loser typically learns to expect mistreatment and regards it as further evidence that abuse is all he or she deserves.

Vince was a thirty-five-year-old father of four. He grew up in the shadow of a father who perpetually bragged about his own "glory days" as a high school athlete and repeatedly maligned his son's lack of aptitude in sports. Because his father's work demanded that the family move frequently, Vince also had difficulty making and keeping friends. Eventually his older brother, Steve, molested him. Vince's sense of isolation made him an easy target. Using his younger brother's lack of friends and parental attention in order to gain his cooperation, Steve made use of the common childhood need for love "at any price."

The Deviate. The Deviate is the child who is repeatedly identified as a "slut," "fag," "retard," "fatso," or "clown." Such children are made to feel hopelessly different in any number of ways. Because of the constant derision, they learn to define their lives in terms of aberration.

From as early as he could remember Derrick was labeled the family "goof ball." His parents laughed at everything he did—even when he wasn't trying to be funny. All of the members of his very large, extended family joined in ridiculing him. They coined the term "The Bozo Award" and awarded it to Derrick every time he did something they regarded as clumsy or inept. Naturally, the boy grew up believing that he would never fit in... that he was destined always to be to awkward and incompetent.

Families find many ways to give their children separate "identities." Not all of them are pleasant or complimentary. Some children are taught that they are a deviate in some "innocent" way—as with Derrick's family. Other children are called a "hot number" or a "flirt" or "fag." Such damaging labels leave children with a dangerously warped image of themselves as a sexual being. Any labeling that causes a child to feel as if he or she is hopelessly different is ultimately destructive.

The Eunuch/Matron. Generally the Eunuch/Matron grows up in a family system in which both parents have been equally abusive or neglectful. Such children feel alienated from both sexes as a result. They feel cut off from their own sexuality and question who they are and where their sexual interests lie. The Eunuch/Matron suffers from severe feelings of isolation. Their isolation then tends to confirm their feeling of being irrevocably different and never belonging.

Roxanne grew up in a severely dysfunctional family. Her father had wanted a son and openly expressed his disappointment over the fact that she was a girl. He abandoned the family when Roxanne was five. Her grandfather who lived with the family was violently abusive toward Roxanne's mother. Meanwhile, her mother beat and publicly shamed all three of her daughters. She also insisted that her daughters strip and remain unclothed around the house for long periods of time. She insisted—well into Roxanne's teens—that the girl bathe with the bathroom door open so that her mother could "peek in on her" whenever she wanted to.

Roxanne learned that being a female was neither desirable nor safe. Her mother's scathing commentary on her femininity caused her to question her femaleness. At the same time, she could never forget how disappointed her father had been that she was a girl. Roxanne grew up knowing that she wasn't entitled to any redeeming male qualities, but felt that being fully female was out of the question.

As a result Roxanne was incapable of bonding with members of either sex. She never developed an interest in boys, but had also chosen to avoid homosexual liaisons. There appeared to be no clear-cut alternative for her. Her dress and demeanor clearly indicated the asexual role she had embraced. Being sexual presented too many conflicts.

WE MUST BE WHO THEY SAY WE ARE

Each of these scripts gives birth to a kind of self-talk that serves to make the assigned role self-perpetuating. If we grow up believing that we are a whore, a fag, an idiot, a coward, a failure, a monster, a weakling, a nuisance, or a troublemaker, we will unconsciously need to live a life congruent with these labels. Our role becomes so well rehearsed that we automatically relate to the world accordingly.

How are we so easily convinced that the role assigned us by our dysfunctional family is the "right" one? A social psychologist, Leon Festinger, provided some insight regarding that question. He argues that human opinion can be altered if the rationale for one's behavior is successfully clouded.

Dr. Festinger conducted a study in which subjects were asked to perform an extremely boring and menial task. The task was presented to the subjects as part of the research design for an experiment. After completing the task themselves, the subjects were instructed to tell potential candidates for the project about the task they had just performed. They were asked to lie to the potential candidates, telling them that the task had been fun and they were sure to enjoy it.

The original subjects were then divided into two groups. The first group was paid twenty dollars to tell the lie. The second group was paid one dollar. When the two groups were interviewed afterward, they were asked, "Was the experiment actually fun?" The subjects who had received twenty dollars for lying willingly admitted that the task was extremely boring. Those who had received only one dollar exhibited a difference of opinion, with a tendency to claim that the task had indeed been fun.

Festinger argued that those subjects who had received a

single dollar for lying felt that the "pay-off" was not enough to justify the lie. They were thus compelled to rationalize the lie in order to live with it. By convincing themselves that the task was fun, they were able to justify their behavior.[1]

The child who is being victimized doubtless feels the stakes are much higher than the subjects of that experiment did. With such a meager pay-off in terms of security and love, the internal conflict created by accepting the lie told by the abuser is nearly overwhelming. In the interest of resolving that conflict and obtaining whatever peace that resolution may afford, the child feels compelled to come to the inevitable conclusion: "I *am* a loser (or deviant, coward, whore, etc.). My behavior proves it."

By believing the lie we are told about our role within our family, we can quiet the inner alarms. Those signals are trying to warn us that what we are receiving in return for playing that role is not enough to justify the humiliation and degradation. The false perceptions we come to believe about ourselves support a kind of self-destructiveness that will continue to imprison us until God's truth sets us free. Meanwhile, Satan works feverishly at keeping our scripts believable. All he has to do is make sure certain tragedies continue to befall us.

The only way out of our dilemma is to replace the lies we have been taught with the truth. We need to establish God's Word in our minds as a replacement for those falsehoods. Scripture tells us that "the mind controlled by the Spirit is life and peace" (Rom 8:6). We also know that God has a beautiful "script" for us as his children, one that invites full participation in his glory. Living out that new script hinges on our willingness to expose our shame and hurt. We must learn what our hearts truly have to say.

THE CHRISTIAN'S SCRIPT

The Christian's script represents God's plan for our lives. It was prepared by a good friend and pastor some years ago.

1. I am a child of God. (Rom 8:15-16; Gal 3:26; 4:6)
2. I am no longer condemned. (Rom 8:1)
3. I am an heir to God's kingdom. (Gal 3:26; Rom 8:17; Jn 1:12; Ti 3:7)
4. I am a member of the kingdom. (Gal 3)
5. I am light. (Mt 5:14)
6. I am salt. (Mt 5:13)
7. I am chosen. (Eph 1:4; Jn 15:16)
8. I am a dwelling place of God. (1 Cor 3:16; 6:19)
9. I am a member of the holy priesthood. (1 Pt 2:4-5)
10. I am a citizen of the kingdom of God and therefore have rights. (Phil 3:20)
11. I am forgiven. (Eph 1:7)
12. I am gifted. (Rom 12:6)
13. I assume a strategic position in the kingdom. (Rom 12:5)
14. I am called. (Eph 4:1)
15. I am a friend of Christ. (Jn 15:14)
16. I have already passed from death to life. (Jn 5:24)
17. I am holy and blameless. (Eph 1:4)
18. I am God's workmanship. (Eph 2:10)

A Practical Exercise

✦ ✦ ✦

Could you see yourself in any of the roles described in this chapter? Or do you feel that you adopted a role other than the ones listed here? The following exercises will help you get in touch with your script.

1. Choose the Scriptures that you feel would most effectively oppose your previous script. Memorize those verses and make it a habit to repeat them to yourself each day.

2. Try to identify habitual responses you have to daily events in your life that reflect the script you adopted as a child. Determine to take the steps outlined below consistently for the next two or three weeks. Once you feel you have broken those habits, choose one or two others to work on. Since breaking habits is difficult and takes time, here are some hints:

a. Take one habit at a time.
b. Find a suitable behavior to replace it.
c. Practice that behavior daily.
d. Forgive yourself for "blowing it."

3. Ask God to help you overcome your previous "scripting" with a prayer like this one:

> *In the authority of the Lord Jesus Christ, whose name is above every name, I declare that I am a child of God and that I share the heritage of his Son. I hereby renounce any role that I may have played in my life until now. I choose, through the power of the Holy Spirit, to live in accordance with God's description of me as a believer and his precious child, as that role is outlined in the Scriptures.*
>
> *I declare that Satan has no power over me. In the name of Jesus, I command you, Satan, and all of your demons to cease your attempts to convince me that I must live out the role I learned as a child. I claim my God-given heritage as provided for me through Christ's death and resurrection, and the coming of the Holy Spirit, who stands with me until Christ's return. Amen.*

SEVEN

Overcoming
Vicious Cycles

I pray that out of his glorious riches he may strengthen you with power through his Spirit in your inner being,... **Ephesians 3:16**

R EBECCA WAS TWENTY-EIGHT years old when she sought my help because of chronic depression and suicidal thoughts. In addition, she suffered from chronic severe headaches and Temporal Mandibular Joint pain (TMJ).

During her first weeks of therapy, Rebecca described a family "held hostage" by her father's unpredictable outbursts of bad temper. Her mother coped by placating him at all costs, enlisting the aid of the entire family in an effort to pacify him. Fear became Rebecca's constant childhood companion as she learned—through her mother's example— how to live with a tyrant.

Rebecca committed her life to the Lord when she was a young adult. Within days of her conversion experience, she was raped by a repairman. The events of that night were both incredible and tragic. The rapist was a complete stranger to her, yet Rebecca passively accepted his invitation to talk with him in his van. In the absence of threats or physical force, she did exactly as she was told, getting into his van without question. It never occurred to her to say no! Her passivity during the event and her emotionless recounting of it in my office seemed significant.

Rebecca told me that the rape must have been "part of God's plan." She thought God wanted her to "prove her love" for him by remaining committed to him in the face of such misfortune. Rebecca's conviction that she must submissively accept the role of a victim in order to gain God's love and approval seemed to me to be a vestige of lessons learned earlier in her life. The question that plagued me was why a child of God would need to prove her love by giving in to rape.

As I worked with Rebecca it became evident that she had a deep distrust of men. Her sense of fearfulness and timidity around men predated her rape. I endeavored to help her recognize the lessons she had learned during her childhood about how to cope with men, and how they had set up a kind of vicious cycle in her life.

Rebecca's mother had repeatedly conveyed the idea that Daddy shouldn't be provoked. He needed to be understood, condescended to, and generally feared. Men were to be treated like ill-tempered and slightly fragile potentates. Further, women were worthless and expendable in this never-ending effort to placate men.

Rebecca learned to accept Daddy's violent temper as stoically as her mother did. Denial became a way of life for her as a result of her mother's insistence that "everyone just ignore" Daddy's frightening, explosive outbursts. She learned to silently accept whatever men might do to her. That was the way to earn their love and approval or—failing that—to avoid still worse treatment or complete abandonment.

TRENCHES WORN OVER TIME

Vicious cycles become entrenched in the thought-life of a victim through repetition. Rebecca's view of men as completely powerful and women as powerless set her up to repeat what she had learned as a child on the night of her rape. In her case the forces of evil called for a repeat of this damaging cycle at precisely the time when her newly proclaimed commitment to God was most easily challenged.

Thirty years ago, S.E. Asch performed an experiment which has become a classic.[1] A group of college students were asked to say which of three lines on a card matched the length of a standard line on a second card. One of the three lines they could choose from was quite obviously the same length as the standard line. The others differed noticeably—some by as much as one and three-quarter inches.

All but one of the students who participated in the experiment at any one time were "plants" who had been instructed to make a unanimously wrong choice. The true subject for the experiment was asked to announce his or her choice only after hearing all of the other students give their wrong choice. The uninitiated students who chose the correct answer did so knowing that they would be standing in opposition to the entire group.

In nearly forty percent of the cases observed, the subject voiced an opinion in agreement with the others. Their desire to conform caused them to dismiss their own perception as faulty and to convince themselves at some level that they did not see what they thought they saw. In other words, these subjects placed more faith in the group than in themselves and willingly allowed their sense of reality to become distorted.

This is a prime example of what takes place in the heart and mind of a victim. Our thoughts are the result of our perceptions, but what we really "see" is based on how we *feel* according to the convictions we hold. Perception is primarily knowledge gained through observation of our environment. Beliefs arise out of a union between these perceptions and our emotions.

When feelings originating from trauma remain unexpressed and unexplored, the resultant misperceptions they bring with them become cast in stone. Thus misbeliefs are born out of a silent retreat from truth. We allow others' perceptions to supersede our own because our emotions tell us that our way of perceiving things is all wrong. Consequently, beliefs about what we must do to be safe in a topsy-turvy world become seeded with lies.

In Asch's experiment, the subjects' underlying belief that their judgment was faulty made it possible to convince them that *their* perception of reality was wrong. Their fear of standing alone—or being abandoned—then provided the motivation to alter their perception so that they would fit in.

In the light of this understanding, we can see how children might "reason" themselves into numerous false beliefs which then give way to vicious cycles. Children whose judgment is constantly invalidated by their caretakers could easily think: "I'm always being yelled at (hit, etc.). No matter what I do, something bad always happens. No one else seems to notice or say anything. I must be seeing things wrong. It must be my fault. I shouldn't get so upset."

And so the forces of evil advance against us by orchestrating experiences that repeatedly point to the same "inevitable" conclusions—tragically altering our reality through the creation and verification of misbeliefs.

I'M VULNERABLE

When we have an underlying belief that we are at risk of further injury—either emotionally or physically—fear of our vulnerability dominates our lives.

Michelle entered therapy because of a rapidly disintegrating marriage and numerous fears that often ended in panic attacks. She was particularly afraid when home alone. Her fear of showering meant that she sometimes avoided bathing. Noises in other rooms sent her into a panic. Michelle was also convinced that she would be assaulted while walking to and from her mailbox.

During the course of her therapy, I learned that Michelle's father had been a low-level drug dealer while she was growing up. Her home had been overrun from time to time by violent criminals who thought nothing of holding a gun to her father's head as they threatened him. When Michelle was ten, her teenage brother had been beaten severely by some of her father's customers. This "object lesson" was intended to drive home the advisability of keeping their mouths shut about who they saw coming and going.

It became apparent to me that the events of her past had set into motion a vicious cycle. As a little girl Michelle had perceived that her powerlessness and resultant vulnerability permitted her victimization and that of her family. She unconsciously generalized her fear because she wasn't allowed to talk about what was happening to her and why. Consequently, fear attached itself to almost every facet of her life. Michelle concluded that she would always be in danger. Her fearfulness crystallized into paranoia, depression, and the need to isolate. The world became a frightening place.

Constant vigilance is the natural result of this cycle. Michelle's wary watchfulness intensified her sense of vulnerability and fear, which further increased her need for vigilance, which further intensified her sense of vulnerability and fear....

I'M POWERLESS

When we come to believe that we are powerless, "learned helplessness" sets in. We live out our lives feeling incapable of facing any new challenge which might force us to assert ourselves. We always see others as more powerful, more significant, and more qualified.

Gordon's father constantly berated him during his childhood. The physical and verbal abuse he suffered at his hands resulted in profound psychological damage. The more his father abused him, the more keenly aware Gordon was of his shortcomings. Because he was never given the opportunity to resolve his feelings of fear by speaking about them, Gordon continued to feel helpless in every situation where he was expected to achieve or assert himself.

As an adult Gordon avoided social situations. He believed that everyone would see him as his father had—worthless. His shame resulted in his isolating himself. When he did venture into the social arena, his relationships always seemed to end in disagreements and misunderstandings.

Gordon's perception of his powerlessness, coupled with his chronic fear of being shamed, produced a robot-like need to defer to others. He gave up his right to be self-directed and deferred to those around him in terms of how he should act and what he should feel. As he did so, Gordon experienced an even greater sense of powerlessness and helplessness. His resulting depression reinforced his feelings of helplessness, causing his fear to increase. And so the cycle continued.

I'M ALONE

As survivors of abuse and neglect, we learn very early in life that other people are not emotionally available to us. We come to the conclusion—either consciously or unconsciously, and always in silence—that we can't count on anyone.

Lyle had a long history of drug abuse. During his childhood his mother had physically abused him whenever his father was absent, always telling him not to let dad know because he would just leave again. He remembered feeling that his father was "never home." Lyle was convinced during much of his childhood that his father would rescue him from his mother's abuse—if only he could prove his worthiness by being helpful around the house. Yet he could never seem to be helpful enough. Lyle's father barely noticed the boy's efforts to repair things and maintain the yard. Finally, during his early adolescence, he gave up all hope of being supported by his father and turned to alcohol.

Lyle had been running from his pain for a long time when he sought my help. He had been married three times. Despite his need to have each of his wives view him as a superhero—a superior bread winner, handyman, emotional support, and so on—Lyle found himself unable to remain faithful to any of them. In addition to his drug abuse, he suffered from sexual addiction that compelled him to have a stream of casual sexual encounters.

Lyle had been emotionally abandoned by his father. Being physically abused in his father's absence further compounded his sense of loss. And the abuser was his mother, the only other person who was "supposed" to care for him. Lyle felt cut off from the world. Seeing no way of escape, he embraced the belief that people he relied on would always abandon him. Having been betrayed by the people who were "supposed" to care most, he recreated the same environment by refusing to allow others to really care for or nurture him.

Lyle's frantic efforts to prevent feelings of abandonment produced a need to avoid being left by anyone. Because his parents had abandoned him, he chose to abandon every relationship before his counterpart could do the same. As a result, Lyle had been emotionally detached all of his adult life. This elicited a growing sense of loneliness and fear. Lyle develpoed a pervasive need to be needed in response to his feeling that he was totally alone and being discounted. But, as he abandoned yet another relationship, Lyle was alone once again.

These three cycles [on page 100] incorporate the most powerful misperceptions common to victims. There are many others. Each of them undermines our efforts to relate to the world around us. They cause us to adopt behaviors that reinforce the thinking that caused us to behave that way in the first place. The chronic behaviors that develop are toxic and create extreme stress. That stress leaves us feeling overwhelmed, which adds to the emotional and social inertia that keeps our self-defeating misperceptions alive.

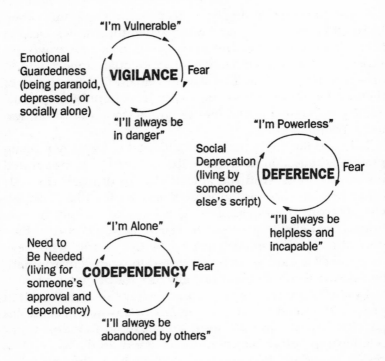

As children we needed to make our lives as simple, safe, and secure as possible. That need has an overriding effect on our belief system. Those beliefs then dictate what we do, how we react, and what we expect whenever uncontrollable events take place in our lives. Because such events translate into a lack of safety, we are willing to adopt a self-defeating behavior in order to make the outcome of any event predictable and therefore "safe."

Even if the outcome we opt for is a painful one, we have at least insured that our existence is simple, safe, and secure. In turn, our moods become predictable and self-fulfilling. Paranoia and depression serve useful purposes. After all, believing we are always in danger prevents us from being taken by surprise. Believing the worst will always happen prevents us from being disappointed. And remaining isolated prevents us from being rejected.

We maintain our illusion of control—and thereby safety—by reducing our expectations to their lowest possible state. However, our hearts find it difficult to become comfortable with the lies we have embraced. We find it necessary to willfully stifle the cry of our hearts in order to make peace with our "solution." As we silence our hearts, we make it possible for the powers of darkness to convince us of even greater lies. And that is the most vicious cycle of all.

Once our life script has told us who we are and what our purpose in life must be, the circumstances that produce these vicious cycles indicate to us what we must do to be safe. Life's three basic questions seen to have been answered.

Because we are never given the opportunity to talk about what has happened to us, our toxic feelings and misperceptions remain bound in silence and our answers all wrong. We focus on our own weaknesses and our efforts to compensate rather than our strength in the Lord. As long as we listen to the lies founded on our past experiences, we remain blind to God's truth about our future.

When we incorporate any lie—even in the form of a misperception—into our lives, we fall prey to forces outside our awareness. These forces are governed by the Father of Lies. Darkness waits to take advantage of every untruth we incorporate into our thinking as evil gains a larger and larger place in the shadows of our mind.

BREAKING THE CYCLE

As we grow, we learn new information based on our perceptions of the world. This data is stored and given meaning according to how psychologically prepared we are to absorb it. When we take in new information, our mind automatically compares it to what is already stored. Then the new information is either stored along with the former information, or recorded as a new bit of information.

When strong emotions resulting from trauma are attached to our perceptions, we are prevented from properly storing any later information derived from life's experiences. We come to the same old conclusions about what has happened and why. From that point in time until those strong emotions are finally expressed and worked through, any situation that we interpret as similar will reawaken those toxic feelings—even when the present situation does not warrant them. Our beliefs will be all wrong about what new events mean.

The similarities between old events (and perceptions) and new situations are called "triggers." If we were frightened as a child by a bull dog and never allowed to work through our feelings, then seeing a dog may reawaken the terror we felt at the time—despite the fact that the present encounter with a dog may be completely unthreatening. In that case, seeing a dog would be a "trigger."

John Bradshaw, in his book, *Bradshaw On: The Family*,[2] uses the metaphor of an "on" switch to explain this phenomenon. Each time we encounter a trigger, we discover the switch to our perceptions is still "on." We are still seeing things in the same old way. An old tape begins to play. Our response simply tells us that some past experience has not been fully dealt with because the present event can't be perceived apart from our past traumatic reference point. New information is consequently never seen as new. It is made similar to old events because our emotion-laden perceptions tell us nothing has changed.

Although our reactions to such triggers may be perplexing, frustrating, and even embarrassing, they can provide a valuable hint as to the nature of our unresolved pain. Expressing the strong emotions resulting from traumatic events will enable us to finally turn the switch to "off." We can then begin to process information properly. Those feelings and their attending perceptions are no longer hidden from our conscious mind, jumbling our thoughts. Our mind's capacity to make sense of events is no longer overwhelmed. We can begin to reorder our thoughts and to answer the question, "What will keep me safe *now*?" It becomes possible to break the vicious cycles.

Change, however, requires more than just expressing our emotions. Old ways of "seeing" things must be recognized and forsaken. The human character is made up of perceptions, feelings, and choices. When taken singly, intellectual assertions, emotional release, or behavior modification will produce little long-term benefit. Lasting change requires that thoughts, feelings, and choices be functioning in concert with one another. And often, in order for this to happen, spiritual hindrance must be overcome.

Humankind was made in God's image. He has fashioned an integrated pattern for our lives that requires heart, soul, and mind to *function* in unison. When they don't, we become *dysfunctional* (see diagram). Satan knows this and works at

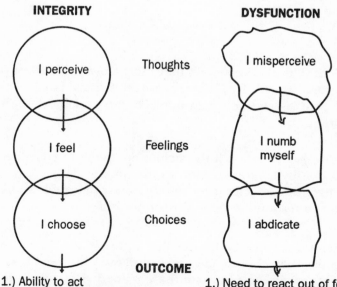

INTEGRITY

I perceive

Thoughts

I feel

Feelings

I choose

Choices

OUTCOME

1.) Ability to act
2.) Ability to surrender to God
3.) Ability to be ourselves

DYSFUNCTION

I misperceive

I numb myself

I abdicate

1.) Need to react out of fear
2.) Need to be in control
3.) Need to 'do' for others

perpetrating our misperceptions. By creating circumstances in our lives that cause us to fear that our perceptions can't be trusted, he succeeds in creating a split between our mind and our heart. We figuratively lose our minds. In convincing us we have no right to our feelings, he creates a split between our heart and our will. We then lose heart. Lastly, we just give up trying to be our true selves.

We need to replace the lies we have believed with the truth. "For as he thinks in his heart, so is he" (Prv 23:7 NKJV). As we make this substitution, we learn to trust God with our emotions—to allow our hearts to speak again. God designed us with emotions. He won't "scold" us for expressing them. As we infuse our thought-life with the truth and vent our suppressed emotions, our choices will begin to reflect the fact that we are new creations in Christ Jesus. Old perceptions will finally give way to a whole *new* way of seeing things.

A Practical Exercise
✦ ✦ ✦

Identify the vicious cycle that most closely describes your emotional world. Don't be surprised if there is more than one. That is extremely common. Then try taking the following steps:

1. Once you know what the vicious cycles are in your life, try to identify habitual responses you have to daily events that reflect those cycles. In what ways are you afraid, and how do you respond to these fears in your life?

2. Memorize some Scriptures that will help you break those habits, then choose one or two and work on them over the next few weeks. Once you have gained victory over those habits, choose one or two more others and work on them.

3. Take a stand against those vicious cycles by praying the following prayer:

In the power of that name which is above every name, Jesus Christ, I rebuke Satan and his lies. I command you, Satan, along with all of your demons, to depart from me. I bring the blood of Jesus Christ between us.

Father, you alone are in control of every event in my life. I renounce fear and claim freedom from its power in the name of your Son, Jesus. I acknowledge that I am not destined always to be in danger. You are my rock and my refuge. In you I am not powerless. You have given me the spirit of love and power and a sound mind. I freely receive those gifts right now.

And I am not alone. You are always present with me in the person of the Holy Spirit. Your eyes are always upon me. Nothing that happens to me escapes your notice. And nothing that has ever happened to me is beyond your healing power. What was meant for evil, God meant for good (Gn 50:20). I claim in Jesus' name release from the bondage of vicious cycles, now and forever. Amen.

EIGHT

Frozen in Time

Then we will no longer be infants, tossed back and forth by the waves, and blown here and there by every wind of teaching.... Instead, speaking the truth in love, we will in all things grow up into him who is the Head, that is, Christ. Ephesians 4:14-15

JOHN HAD BEEN STRUGGLING WITH sexual compulsion for years when he entered therapy. Although happily married, he constantly fought the urge to masturbate whenever his wife was away or after she had gone to bed. Wanting to pursue his private sexual activity without hindrance, John's compulsive masturbation had figured prominently in his decision to leave his first marriage. He was concerned that he might make the same mistake with his second marriage if he didn't get help.

John grew up in a home where both parents were alcoholics. Their constant, unnerving bickering had been a dominant thread in the fabric of his young life. John described his father as uninvolved and emotionally distant. Even when his father was physically present, he spent most of his time shut away from the family, working in the garage.

John made frequent childlike efforts to enter his father's mysterious world by attempting to build things in the garage along with him. Each of his attempts met only scorn and criticism. John's father invariably dismantled his building projects and reassembled them "correctly." Eventually, the boy abandoned his futile efforts to measure up. Continually frustrated by his inability to win his father's love, he quite naturally felt that God must be equally distant and lacking in acceptance of him.

John's mother was subject to crying jags. Her despair left John feeling helpless and frustrated by his inability to "save" her and his father. His brother was the "superhero" of the household. John's memory of growing up in his brother's shadow was still painful. As a child, he always felt like a burden—an unwelcome addition to his family.

In seventh grade one of John's friends invited him to spend the night at his house. George took the opportunity to introduce his friend to the act of masturbation. He talked John into disrobing in front of him. John reluctantly did so, but then his friend wanted to touch him as well. Because John didn't realize he had the right to say no, he submitted. He walked away from the experience a profoundly different human being.

Some days later George announced to the kids at their lunch table at school that John had talked *him* into undressing and masturbating with him. He labeled John a "queer." George proceeded to describe to everyone listening how "small" John's penis was, remarking that he could never be a "real man." John was shattered. He didn't feel good about his body or his sexuality from then on.

But Satan had only just begun his plan for John's destruction. Six months later John's father decided to introduce his sons to the "pleasures" of pornography. John's mother protested loudly, but remained too impotent to do more than yell and pout. John was overjoyed to finally find himself a part of his father's world. At last, he had the relationship with his father he had always longed for. He learned from his father that the enjoyment of pornography made him a "real man."

Some might argue that these two separate events could not possibly be tied together by anything more substantial than coincidence. We know that our enemy, the devil, "prowls around like a roaring lion looking for someone to devour" (1 Pt 5:8). Peter's analogy is a good one. Lions are cunning predators. The male lion often flushes its prey out of hiding by roaring loudly. The frightened animals rush headlong into the waiting jaws of the females of the pride who lie in wait.

In John's case, George had supplied the roar through his public and shameful declaration. John's shame in addition to his intense desire to have a relationship with his father caused the boy to run headlong into the trap of pornography and compulsive masturbation.

The pain and defeat that overtook John as a result of these events is ample proof that they emanated from the powers of darkness. Just as God has a plan for our life, Satan has a plan for our destruction. The ultimate outcome of Satan's plan was determined through the death and resurrection of our Lord and Savior, Jesus Christ. But it is up to us to fight our individual battles with the spiritual knowledge God makes available to us.

In John's case, his father's emotional distance "set him up" to be victimized by any male who might give him attention. That same lack provided him a compelling reason to enter into his father's sordid activities. John's need to come to terms with his increasingly evident sexuality was complicated by his misperception that there was something questionable about him as a male. His father supplied the "answer" in the form of the lie: "This will make you a man." When John masturbated, he "proved" his manhood.

As a result of these experiences, John suffered what's called a "developmental arrest" during adolescence. His perceptions, feelings, and beliefs had been frozen at that moment—almost as if they had been placed in a time capsule. Until he examined the contents of his personal time capsule, John was unable to successfully move through the stages that were to follow.

A DEVELOPMENTAL TIMETABLE

According to Dr. Erik Erikson, humans pass through eight stages of growth and development between birth and death.[1] When a traumatic event causes an arrest of emotional development during any one of the stages, all succeeding stages are built upon that faulty stage. As with any structure placed on a faulty foundation, our emotional growth becomes lopsided and easily shaken.

Five of these stages are experienced during the first twenty years of life. The other three take place during adulthood. Erikson observed that each stage represents a "psychosocial crisis" or turning point, when both potential for growth and vulnerability to arrest are immense. When we remember specific traumatic events and our age at the time, we can determine rather easily where our developmental breaks occurred.

It is also possible to determine when those breaks occurred from our behavior—even in the absence of concrete memories. In either case, we can use Erikson's stage theory to see how the enemy has caused us to run into the jaws of relational difficulties that can leave us feeling defeated as Christians.

Stage one: trust versus mistrust (infancy to two years). The milestone negotiated in this stage is called "symbiosis." A newborn is completely dependent upon his or her caretakers. When love and nurturance are consistently given, that child learns that it is safe to trust and "okay" to have needs.

In an unhealthy environment where care and nurturance are withheld or given sporadically, we learn that it is not safe to trust. Our neediness makes us feel vulnerable or "unsafe." We learn that our needs aren't "okay." As a result, we cut ourselves off from others and have extreme difficulty bonding. We tend to grow up feeling suspicious of others, aloof, and incapable of establishing the most basic relational skills. This behavior—as with all the others that occur as the result of developmental breaks—tends to be self-perpetuating. We grow up isolating and refusing to test our assumption that "no one can be trusted."

Some of the characteristics and misbeliefs that develop as a result of a stage one arrest are:

1. Difficulty in asking for help or emotional support.
2. A belief that no one will ever be there for us.
3. An assumption that people are "bad," not trustworthy, out to get us, or only want to know "what's in it" for them.
4. A tendency to focus on others' faults.
5. A tendency to be guarded and overly sensitive.
6. An inability to control our urges, often resulting in compulsive behaviors.
7. A belief that there may not be "enough" for me, with a resultant difficulty in sharing what we have.
8. An inability to be self-disclosing.
9. A tendency toward pessimism or chronic dissatisfaction.
10. A tendency toward blaming or projection.
11. A tendency toward isolationism.
12. Generalized fear or anxiety.
13. Hyper-vigilance.
14. Regressive behaviors when stressed.
15. Using illness as a reason to be cared for.

Stage two: autonomy versus shame and doubt (age two to four). The milestone negotiated during this stage is called "separation." We are moving toward a social and emotional mastery of our immediate environment. Our sense of independence from our caretakers is increasing. We venture further from them and explore our surroundings more freely.

Healthy, nurturing parents will encourage us to stand on our own feet. They will provide firm, loving control of the tendency toward anarchy that results from our lack of maturity. They will provide us with the opportunity to make nonessential choices so that we can experience the decision-making process and learn to have confidence in our decisions. A sense of confident autonomy develops in such a family.

In a detrimental environment, we experience shaming used as a punishment, the suppression of self-expression, and overcontrol. These child-rearing mistakes leave us with a chronic feeling of guilt and a sense of continually falling short. We also experience a marked lack of free choice, even in minor matters. We encounter continual criticism of our self-help efforts. The criticism may be either open scorn or a "Here honey, let me do it for you" variety. We are either over-protected or "left to the wolves." These experiences result in strong doubt as to our ability to cope in the world.

A stage two arrest can result in the following characteristics:

1. Overdependence in relationships.
2. Expecting misfortune to follow whenever we feel good.
3. A fixation on our own improprieties.
4. A tendency to be "other-related."
5. A preference for being told what to do.
6. An inability to say no.
7. A tendency to live according to "shoulds" and "oughts."
8. A tendency to be easily dominated.
9. Black and white thinking.
10. A tendency to be easily embarrassed.
11. Chronic worry and self-doubt.
12. Chronic idealization of others.
13. A tendency to love/hate relationships.
14. Difficulty letting go.
15. A constant search for heroes or saviors.

Stage three: initiative versus guilt (age four to seven). The milestone in this stage is called "primary identity," when we are developing self-motivation and the desire to be in control of our destiny. In a healthy family, parents provide us with opportunities to plan and carry out activities. We develop confidence in our ability to plan and attack a task.

In an unhealthy environment, we are inhibited from undertaking tasks and experience derision of our abilities in this area. As a result, we develop anxiety about our abilities and frequently develop a fear of "bungling" tasks, leading to overcontrol and constriction of our activities in adulthood.

John's case is a perfect example of this kind of developmental arrest. His efforts to enter his father's world were constantly denigrated. His work was consistently devalued. Each time his father dismantled and reassembled one of his building projects, the message he received was that he was inadequate, incompetent, and hopeless.

Arrests in this stage result in these kinds of behaviors:

1. An unwillingness to take risks.
2. The assumption of blame for every failure.
3. Becoming the classic "underachiever."
4. An inability to get anything done or to set goals.
5. Resistance to new challenges.
6. Being rigidly moralistic.
7. Inertia—someone else must always tell us how to get started.
8. Fear of "rocking the boat."
9. Constantly feeling guilty or feeling the need to try harder.
10. Constant procrastination.
11. Fear of disapproval, failure, ridicule, or rejection.
12. Unwillingness to take a leadership role.
13. Needing others to tell us how or what to feel.
14. Constantly apologizing.
15. Perfectionism.

Stage four: industry versus inferiority (age seven to twelve). The milestone in stage four is called "socio-ability." At this stage we struggle not only with our need to complete a task but also with the fruitfulness of our efforts. We have a great desire to be useful or to produce a useful product.

During this stage parents need to give clear and systematic instruction, recognize our product or service, and applaud its usefulness. They also need to provide opportunities for non-family members to recognize and appreciate our industry. Given such positive experiences, we will develop enjoy-

ment in applying ourselves to a given task and a sense of satisfaction in a job well done. We also begin to comprehend the
need to share or divide labor.

If the family fails to teach us healthy ways to relate to adults
and children in school and the broader world, then an arrest
can occur at this stage. Or the school may fail to provide a
safe, healthy environment. Or an arrest can occur if we repeatedly have cause to believe that external factors play a
larger role in determining the worth of our labor than our
own efforts do. Here, again, John's case provides a good example. Because his work was criticized, he came to believe
that his effort had little or nothing to do with the end result of
any undertaking—regardless of the herculean effort he
made.

Arrests at this stage of development typically result in the
following characteristics:

1. Rebellious or antisocial behavior.
2. Playing it safe, nonproductivity, or a fear of failing to
   produce.
3. Being loud and distracting or being a clown.
4. Lack of curiosity or desire to learn new things.
5. Hating to begin new projects.
6. Poor learning ability.
7. Compensating for feelings of inferiority by being a brag-
   gart or daredevil.
8. An inability to take criticism.
9. An inability to complete things, or sabotaging our
   efforts so that we will have an excuse not to produce.
10. Compensating by building a reputation for being bright
    and logical or being seen as an intellectual.
11. Feelings of inadequacy or rationalizing our failures.
12. Constantly second guessing ourselves.
13. Not wanting anyone to notice us or feeling conspicuous.
14. Constant feelings of a lack of acceptance.
15. Constant need to be thinner, prettier, or better looking.

Stage five: identity versus diffusion (adolescence). The milestone in stage five is called "secondary identity." In healthy surroundings, we come to terms with who we are and develop a sense of self during this stage. We begin to understand that we are not the center of the universe and do not necessarily cause every event in our lives.

When we are in a healthy atmosphere at this stage, we will have our self-image validated both as a human being and as a male or female. We will be assisted in accepting our weaknesses and will be provided the opportunity to pursue activities in keeping with our strengths. Ideally, we will be provided with appropriate role models of both genders and will begin to interact with the opposite sex. We will develop a strong enough sense of identity that we can "let life happen." We won't go through life assuming that anything that goes wrong is a reflection on us as an individual. We learn to see beyond what we do to who we are.

In an unhealthy environment, we will have our sense of identity undermined—both as a member of our sex and as a worthwhile human being. Often, we will seek to compensate for such a lack through over-identification with heroes or members of our "crowd." Because his parents were alcoholics, John lacked appropriate role models of either sex. He was therefore extremely vulnerable to the judgment of his crowd at school. Similar situations make us feel that circumstances, rather than our inherent worth, dictate our value. We continue to believe that circumstances dictate whether or not God loves us today.

An arrest at this stage can result in these behaviors:

1. Chronic worrying.
2. Thrill seeking.
3. Overachieving.
4. Compulsiveness, rigidity, or perfectionism—feeling a desperate need to be "right."
5. Setting many goals without a long-range plan.

6. Difficulty getting close to people.
7. Indecisiveness—fearing a wrong decision so much that we make none.
8. A critical or cynical attitude.
9. Becoming fatalists, feeling "It's out of my hands."
10. A self-concept determined by how well we are "producing."
11. Being unable to define what we want or how we fit in.
12. Having lots of ideas with an inability to put them into action.
13. Perpetual adolescence or an unwillingness to grow up.
14. Lack of ambition, being easily distracted or dissatisfied, or bored.
15. A need to be considered "one of the guys" or wanting to be like everyone else.

Stage six: intimacy versus isolation (young adulthood). The milestone of this stage is called "union." When intimacy is fostered, we learn to be committed to a partnership and develop the internal strength to maintain that commitment. An arrest occurs when young adults experience exploitation, abuse, or competitiveness rather than a mutuality of efforts and cooperativeness. We then tend toward isolation, avoid commitment, and become self-absorbed.

Behaviors that tend to develop as the result of an arrest at this stage are:

1. Being everyone's friend but no one's lover.
2. An inability to wholly give one's self to someone else.
3. An unwillingness to adapt for the common good or an inability to compromise.
4. "Hyper" independence.
5. Feeling "out of control" when attempting to enter into a committed relationship.
6. An unwillingness to settle down.
7. Feeling that commitment results in being "stuck."
8. Difficulty in distinguishing "wanting" from "needing" someone.

intamacy is self-revelation.

9. Feeling that being united with someone means needing to fight continually for our rights.
10. Believing that "giving in" is equal to "giving up."
11. Having many acquaintances but no intimate friendships.
12. Going from one relationship to another.
13. Continual need to be the "center" of any relationship.
14. Believing that commitment means forfeiting self.
15. An unwillingness to ask people for what we need.

Since this book is for survivors of childhood abuse and neglect, it is unnecessary to delve into the final two stages identified by Erikson. However, for those who are interested, stage seven spans the thirties and forties: generativity versus stagnation. Stage eight during the fifties and early sixties is termed ego integrity versus despair.

Dr. Erikson observed that everyone is molded by both positive and negative experiences in each stage. Our ability to cope with later stages is better when the ratio is more positive than negative. However, he also noted that some negative experiences may be helpful. For example, a certain degree of mistrust prevents us from being gullible and creates a healthy cautiousness. A certain readiness to experience shame or doubt helps people choose to behave appropriately. The capacity to feel guilty helps people make correct moral judgments and behave responsibly toward others.

When development proceeds normally with no outstanding traumatic events to derail its progress, the attitude of basic trust that develops during stage one helps us feel safe enough to expand the range and diversity of our experiences. In the process, we develop an appropriate autonomy in stage two. Trusting our environment and feeling a necessary autonomy reinforces the attitude or initiative associated with stage three. This freedom encourages the industry of stage four. When the basic groundwork is laid, we are ready for the monumental challenge of stage five—establishing a sense of identity. The results are an essentially positive self-concept.

Each stage builds upon the previous stage. A breakdown at any stage greatly increases the risk of breaks in later stages. But we can be sure that God can and will transform us. We have his promise that we "are being transformed into his likeness with ever-increasing glory, which comes from the Lord" (2 Cor 3:18).

A MODEL FOR RECOVERY

By now you will probably have a fairly good idea—based on your recognition of the symptoms listed at the end of each stage description—where the developmental breaks occurred in your life. The answers to the following questions can further help you to identify your own arrests.

1. Do I feel able to count on anyone? (stage one)
2. Do I feel safe about leaving? (stage two)
3. Am I "okay" if I fail sometimes? (stage three)
4. Do I know what I am capable of doing? (stage four)
5. Do I know who I am? (stage five)
6. Can I commit? (stage six)

In order to recover from the traumatic events that helped to shape us, we need to do the following:

Take responsibility for solving our problem. Yes, someone wronged us. But we are the ones with the problem. We need to acknowledge that we are choosing to *remain* alone, dependent, irresponsible, inconsistent, and uncommitted. It is up to us to take responsibility for our recovery, secure in the knowledge that we are not alone. God is with us.

Define the problem. Once we have identified the areas where we have suffered an arrest in our developmental process, we can define our needs more accurately. Then, with God's help, we are able to see that those needs are met.

Ask God for help in overcoming our past. God has proved himself faithful in the lives of countless thousands of victims throughout history. He will never leave us or forsake us (see

Ask God to define himself in his many ways.

Dt 31:6). David was described as a man after God's own heart. He said, "Though my father and mother forsake me, the LORD will receive me. Teach me your way, O LORD; lead me in a straight path because of my oppressors.... I am still confident in this: I will see the goodness of the LORD in the land of the living. Wait for the LORD; be strong and take heart and wait for the LORD" (Ps 27:10-11, 13-14). We too can rest in the assurance that we will see the goodness of the Lord in the land of the living.

Find the appropriate people to help us. The group process can be very helpful here. The handicaps common to survivors are all relational. We have difficulty relating to God, to ourselves, and to others. It makes sense for us to enter into relationships that can provide us with a "classroom" in which we can replace our past negative experiences with positive ones. Our positive experiences with others help us repair our developmental breaks. As each break is healed, we will find ourselves maturing. Our perceptions and our emotions will begin to reflect each new, more advanced developmental stage.

I especially recommend therapy groups run by responsible, aware therapists like Parents United—for those who suffered sexual abuse as children and the parents of children who have been sexually abused. Private therapy groups can also be very helpful, as well as Twelve Step groups such as Alcoholics Anonymous, Narcotics Anonymous, Overeaters Anonymous, Adult Children of Alcoholics, Survivors of Incest Anonymous, Codependents Anonymous (sometimes called "CoDA").

Many churches have these groups meeting on their premises both with and without church sponsorship. If you feel more comfortable in a therapy group run by Christian therapists, by all means try to find one. However, many non-Christian groups—providing they are are not actually anti-Christian—provide extremely worthwhile experiences.

Expect the recovery process to be painful. In order to *recover*, we must *uncover*. The process necessarily includes uncovering pain, grief, anger, and fear. It is helpful to keep in mind that those feelings have been hidden within us all along. We are not introducing those feelings into our lives, merely exposing them to God's healing light.

Expect to "fail." This may sound like a defeatist attitude, but it isn't. We can slow our progress by expecting to make major strides simply as the result of identifying our recovery needs. The identification of those needs is simply a first step. Expect to take many, many "baby" steps for some while.

Our progress can seem excruciatingly slow in the beginning. We must allow ourselves the luxury of failing. We will learn as much or more from our "mistakes" or "failures" as we do from our successes. God's "grace is sufficient for you, for [his] power is made perfect in weakness" (2 Cor 12:9).

Develop the habit of seeing yourself as God sees you. We are perfected in Jesus Christ. We are already victors and have access to the throne of grace through Jesus Christ. If we can learn to go easy on ourselves, we will make faster progress. If we can see ourselves in the process of "becoming" rather than as we are at this moment, we will be kicking the supports out from under one more of Satan's lies: "It's hopeless, I'll never make it."

Don't believe it. There is hope in all our tomorrows. When we accepted Jesus Christ as our Savior, God began his work in us. Philippians 1:6 tells us that you can be "confident in this, that he who began a good work in you will carry it to completion until the day of Christ Jesus." You will make it. It just takes time.

Continually invite God to be part of your recovery process. Through prayer, through the application of God's Word, and by inviting God to reveal truth to our spirits, we consciously acknowledge that God is at work in our recovery. When we remind ourselves that God is orchestrating the events of our lives in order to promote our healing, our recovery progresses more quickly than it otherwise would.

One of my clients recovered a repressed memory the day before her weekly therapy group was scheduled to meet. Becky was in the midst of dealing with the emotions connected with that memory when she arrived at her meeting the following evening. After attending this particular group for more than a year, events went very badly and group members began shouting at one another. Chaos reigned for a few minutes.

That evening's group process duplicated—on an emotional level—the traumatic event Becky had just remembered the day before. She experienced again the fear, grief, anger, and feelings of helplessness that resulted in a kind of paralysis or inability to "save" herself.

Then the therapist in charge intervened. He invited Becky to process those feelings with him. In that instant her history was "rewritten"—again, on an emotional level. Becky was "saved" from what she perceived to be a parallel experience. A vicious cycle was halted because she was able to talk about her fearfulness.

When she had the opportunity to calm herself and think through what had happened, Becky could see that—even though the experience had been extremely uncomfortable for her—God's hand was evident in the events of that evening. He had taken the opportunity to replace a negative formative experience with a positive one. I have repeatedly witnessed similar occurrences in the lives of Christians who are trusting God with their recovery process. The results are often miraculous.

Learn to be "real." We have probably attempted to hide the handicaps that have resulted from our developmental arrests. We need to abandon any such attempts. This, of course, is a trust issue. When we lack trust, then we will usually suffer from generalized fearfulness, blaming and projection, isolationism, chronic dissatisfaction, hypervigilance, and even panic attacks.

While trust is the issue, it has a lot more to do with whether or not we trust God than it does whether we trust our fellows. When we learn to trust God, we find that we can risk being "real." After all, if God is for us, who can be against us?

IDENTIFYING THE LIES

Overcoming each of our developmental arrests will become easier if we are able to identify the lie we have believed in response to the events that caused our arrests. A stage one arrest, resulting in the inability to trust, is usually accompanied by misbeliefs like these: "No one can be trusted." "I'm safer alone." "Bonding with another human being is an impossible dream."

Given the incapacity to achieve autonomy or separation, which results from a stage two arrest, we tend to believe that: "My safety depends on remaining dependent." "Setting personal boundaries is dangerous because it separates me from others."

A couple of the lies that accompany a stage three arrest resulting in a lack of initiative are: "People won't like me if I take the initiative." "I'm not safe unless I wait for someone else to tell me what to do."

Untruths we believe as a result of a stage four arrest, where our industriousness is undermined, tend to be: "My work and I are one and the same. When someone criticizes my work, they criticize me." "Nothing I do will ever be good enough. Why try?"

As a result of the absence of a clear-cut identity, which is a reflection of a stage five arrest, we come to these kinds of wrong conclusions: "I don't know who I am." "If I admit I'm wrong I'm admitting I'm no good."

If we are unable to commit to another person, as a result of a developmental break in stage six, we think: "I have to give up *me* in order to love *you*." "If I commit to the service of God, I'll have to give up everything I want and everything I am."

Ascribing to such lies keeps us relationally handicapped,

incapable of enjoying the fullness of God's grace within the fellowship of believers. Our woundedness results in mistrust, misunderstanding, and misuse of one another. The church then becomes just another dysfunctional family.

When we see God as loving and sovereign, we find it easier to trust him and one another. We are able to rest in God's goodness as we hack away at the falsehoods in our lives with the sword of truth. We can rest in the knowledge that nothing that happens to us is out of God's control. Nothing has taken him by surprise. God has promised to use the events of our lives to build us up and to help us to better reflect his Son, Jesus Christ.

When we view things in this way, we can begin to accept our "mistakes" or "failures" more philosophically. We can look for the good that we can be sure will come out of them. We can choose to learn from every circumstance in our lives.

And we know that in all things God works for the good of those who love him, who have been called according to his purpose. For those God foreknew he also predestined to be conformed to the likeness of his Son, that he might be the firstborn among many brothers. And those he predestined, he also called; those he called, he also justified; those he justified, he also glorified. Rom 8:28-30

Expecting too much, too soon, defeats our efforts. Expecting too little of ourselves keeps us from growing. We need to approach each new phase of our recovery with prayer and a genuine desire to become all that God wants us to be. Along with that desire, we need the assurance that God sees us as already perfected. Our place with him is guaranteed.

Being continually mindful of God's sovereignty allows us to accept the pace at which we are able to grow. It also affords us the self-acceptance to openly admit the handicaps that have resulted from our developmental arrests. When we know that we are completely accepted by God just as we are, we are enabled to separate ourselves from the lies that we have believed. When we openly admit our shortcomings, we invite God to perfect his strength in our weakness (see 2 Cor 12:9). Such a stance also allows us the courage to confess our shortcomings, fears, and secret shame. We know that we are confessing to a loving Father who only wants to help us overcome them.

The shame of a secret that remains in hiding provides a foothold for Satan. Frequently, our shame stems from a milestone experience—a traumatic event frozen in time through the act of repression. It holds within it the kernel of our shame, and much of our shame-based behavior is founded on it. Once we have openly admitted our secret and confessed whatever wrong we feel may have been our responsibility—whether legitimate or not—we will be free from that milestone shame.

Many of us feel shame over the fact that our bodies responded pleasurably when we were molested. We may feel shame over having supplanted our mother or father in the life of his or her spouse. We feel shame over our anger, our childish plans for revenge, our loss of innocence and purity. The list can seem endless.

Many of these things were simply not our fault, but the shame and guilt we feel as a result of our experiences is nonetheless real. Once we have confessed all of it to our Daddy-God, we have deprived Satan of one of his strongholds in our lives. We are free to admit our anger, move on to grief and, finally, to healing.

RECOVERY CHECKLIST

Once you know the relational issues that most hinder you, you can begin to explore ways to overcome them. Is it trust, autonomy, initiative, industry, identity, or intimacy? You most likely struggle with more than one of these issues. Choose to work first on the issue that developed earliest in your life.

Here is a checklist to aid you in your recovery. First, read through these statements. Resolve to do each one as you become ready.

- Take responsibility for solving this problem.
- Confess all my secrets to God.
- Promise to seek help and not to go it alone.
- Pray daily, inviting God to show me in what ways I need to change and how.
- Search the Scriptures each day to seek a fuller knowledge of the truth.
- Accept the fact that I will have setbacks or "failures" in the course of my recovery and that's okay. I will learn from them, too.
- Do my best to keep a daily log in order to track the progress I make in whatever area I happen to be working on. For example, if I am working on trust issues, then each day I will log whom I have trusted and in what ways.

We need to truly believe—way down inside of our hearts—that God is sovereign. Once we do, we are better prepared to watch in awe as God takes whatever "junk" has been dumped on us as children and recycles it in a divine way. We can become a witness to the world by allowing God to make something beautiful of our lives.

What good can possibly come from our affliction? Paul had the answer: "And we rejoice in the hope of the glory of God. Not only so, but we also rejoice in our sufferings, because we know that suffering produces perseverance; perseverance, character; and character, hope. And hope does not disappoint us, because God has poured out his love into our hearts by the Holy Spirit, whom he has given us" (Rom 5:2-5).

As we allow God to "re-parent" us, we can begin to appreciate the miraculous things God is accomplishing in our lives over time. We will begin to see that God is really there for us, and that he always has been. We will finally know that he is, indeed, our Daddy-God.

A Practical Exercise

✦ ✦ ✦

1. Divide a piece of paper into two columns. Make a list of as many things as you can remember that caused you to feel shame as a child. In the opposite column, list the ways you attempted to hide your shame.

2. Mark with a star or check each of the shame-covering habits you still practice. Using the recovery checklist, begin to work at giving these things up to the Lord.

3. Pray the following prayer:

> *Lord, I confess to you the ways I have tried and still try to cover my shame [list them]. I ask that you forgive me for [list any of the ways that are contrary to God's Word]. Lord, remove my shame. Heal my brokenness. Open my eyes so that I may see any other ways in which I may not have trusted you fully. Show me the ways Satan is hindering me and lying to me.*
>
> *I command the spirit of shame to depart from me in the name of the Lord Jesus Christ. I take a stand right now against all the accusations of Satan. I cover myself in the blood of Jesus and claim my right through his shed blood to stand holy and blameless before the throne of grace.*

NINE

The Need to Be Needed

Because you are sons, God sent the Spirit of his Son into our hearts, the Spirit who calls out, "Abba, Father." So you are no longer a slave, but a son; and since you are a son, God has made you also an heir. Galatians 4:6-7

HARRY WAS TWENTY-EIGHT years old, the "prisoner" of a stormy marriage of three years. He had grown up in a rigidly moral household where weakness and feelings were never permitted. In response to his parents' unwillingness to acknowledge his emotional pain, he had developed more and more physical aches and pains.

When Harry came to see me, he was also suffering from compulsive behaviors such as overeating, compulsive spending, and workaholism. His parents were workaholics and extremely religious. Their legalistic insistence on his absolute compliance left him fearful and placating. In an effort to win his parents' approval, he had become a perfectionist.

Harry felt that his mother's insistence on keeping the "nicest house in the neighborhood" left him with no recourse but to win her approval by becoming a "good little worker." His father had been successful at practically everything, but his workaholism had cheated Harry of the time and attention he needed.

During his early years, Harry also believed he was in danger of being rejected by his parents because of their stern, unbending attitude toward him. As all children do, he needed his parents. Fear caused him to set about securing a place for himself within his family system by making himself indispensable. He needed to be needed in order to feel safe.

In his loneliness, the boy had turned increasingly to fantasy. He had spent much of his childhood dreaming of the perfect, happy family he would have one day. He would be successful at everything, just like his father. And his wife would keep a spotless house, just like his mother. She would appreciate his efforts as a breadwinner and they would have a truly loving home.

As a child, Harry had developed an unconscious understanding that perfection equaled safety. As an adult, his awareness of his lack of control over unfolding events created a pervasive need to regain that control. He felt so inadequate and out of control that he was perplexed over the fact that other people frequently described him as "a bully."

As a married man, Harry continued to be locked in a dependent relationship with his parents. He visited them weekly and continued to take their criticisms very seriously. Still desperately seeking their approval, he never failed to consult them regarding any decision pertaining to his life, marriage, or job.

Harry was hypercritical of others, especially his wife, which indicated to me that he carried a reservoir of submerged anger. At work, Harry was a chameleon. While he made herculean efforts to keep his boss pacified, he also demanded perfection of those he supervised. Harry's identity was determined by the "signals" he picked up from those around him. He became alternately passive-aggressive, passive-dependent, and a demanding perfectionist—according to what he thought was expected of him and by whom.

In time Harry was able to see that he had embraced several misconceptions as a result of the unhappy events of his childhood. He adopted perfectionism in a constant effort to prove that he wasn't bad. He came to believe that his safety hinged on giving people what they wanted, just as his parents insisted he do.

During the course of his treatment, Harry became a member of a therapy group. It became apparent that he was not going to be able to relinquish the false sense of security his codependent behavior afforded him until he saw clearly how constricting it was. His desire for the "safety" his behavior seemed to provide was greater than his need to be free.

The psychological terms used to describe this phenomenon are *egosyntonic* and *egodystonic.* An *egosyntonic* behavior is one that is acceptable to the ego—the ego being defined as the decision-making part of one's being. Therapists often try by various means to cause a previously egosyntonic behavior to become *egodystonic*—no longer acceptable to the ego.

Like all survivors, Harry had invested himself in the task of remaining safe in a terrifying, out-of-control world. He needed to develop a gut-level perception of what his perceived "safety" cost. I decided that a metaphorical demonstration of the constriction in his life might bring the truth home to him. Metaphor is an invaluable therapy tool.

During the group therapy, we asked Harry to review in detail the abuses he had suffered as a child. While he recounted these events, the co-facilitators in the group wrapped Harry in masking tape from head to toe. The tape represented the lies he had embraced as a child. The lie that he could win security through self-sufficiency and successful manipulation of others had to be replaced with the truth regarding his pain and grief.

As Harry stood wrapped from head to foot, the group encouraged him to voice his discomfort and yell out his desire to be set free. Once he had experienced on a feeling level the constriction he had only known thus far on a thinking level, Harry became more willing to abandon his codependence. The group applauded him as he tore himself free of his confinement. Harry was finally able to take more serious steps toward Christ-dependency. After some months of therapy, he was able to say with greater conviction, "I am secure in the family of God and that is all I need."

THE SURVIVAL GAME

A dysfunctional family almost inevitably fosters a desperate need to be needed in all of its members. Melody Beattie, author of *Co-Dependent No More*,[1] tells us that codependence results from the failure of our families to marshal the emotional resources necessary to adequately nurture and emotionally sustain us.

A few years ago, the First National Forum on Codependency in Phoenix named a twenty-person panel to come up with an acceptable definition of codependency. The result of five hours of effort was this: "A pattern of painful dependence upon compulsive behaviors and on approval from others in an attempt to find safety, self-worth, and identity."[2]

As children in a dysfunctional family, we come to the conclusion that being a perfectionist or a "rescuer" will magically alleviate the family's craziness. We develop behaviors which are overly compliant and hypervigilant. No matter how crazy our family system is, our instincts tell us that our survival depends on fitting in and being needed within that family unit. We create a false sense of safety for ourselves by becoming indispensable. We come to the conclusion that we dare not have any needs or wants of our own. We muffle the cries of our hearts and stuff down the pain we feel.

In our urgency to prevent our family from abandoning us, we abandon ourselves. Reversing God's plan for the family as a place where children's needs for nurturance and safety are met, we scramble to provide nurturance and safety for our families. We learn to play the survival game. *Every* thought, *every* word, *every* action is based on our belief that we must control *every* encounter and *every* relationship if we are to remain safe. Our need to be needed provides fertile soil in which compulsive behaviors and obsessive thinking can grow.

Dysfunctional families demand secrecy. In subtle ways and

ways not so subtle, it is communicated to us that we must never openly acknowledge the craziness around us. We are told, "This is a family problem, we'll handle it ourselves. It's no one else's business." Or, "It's not really so bad. Lots of kids have it much worse. What have you got to complain about? Why can't you ever be grateful for what you have?" When we voice a need for safety or love, we may hear, "Why are you so selfish? Can't you ever think of anyone besides yourself?"

All of these messages produce a socially condoned and expedient form of insanity. Our internal sense of reality—our feelings and perceptions about the events around us—is forfeited for the "greater good." We are taught that wanting something for ourselves, no matter how small, is selfish. We learn to feel ashamed of the fact that we have needs.

Shame and fear are the roots of codependent behavior. From those roots grows a trunk of anger—an anger that we dare not acknowledge, because we sense that we are not so indispensable that we could ever dare to show our anger. Besides, if we are not supposed to be selfish enough to have needs, then we certainly mustn't be selfish enough to be angry when those needs aren't met. We wave our magic wand—a product of our childlike trust and desperate need—and poof! our anger disappears.

But of course, our anger doesn't actually disappear. All we have really done is transmute it into compulsive and self-destructive behaviors. Our hearts become walled in by toxic emotions and misbeliefs. As the need to become "numb" in order to win approval overwhelms our need to express our emotions, we live out our lives with emotional turbulence roiling just beneath the surface. In facing the rigors of life, we will—more often than not—return to that which is familiar, and therefore "secure." This often means choosing a marriage partner who will perpetuate our dysfunctional family system.

Eventually we become convinced that our own sense of reality is wrong. We consistently supplant our own reality with the "reality" of others. At the same time we are placing our trust in someone else's concept of reality, we are completely unable to trust anyone else for our safety. We grew up in families where it was "every man for himself." The burden of providing for our own safety has been ours for too long. And because trusting others is so difficult for us, we find it equally difficult to trust God.

Our dysfunctional family system teaches us that our thoughts and feelings are invalid. We conclude not only that we have no intrinsic value, but that our own judgment is faulty. Because we can't trust even ourselves, we don't try to make judgments about what is right or wrong anymore. We simply accept the opinion of those around us. Then we become vulnerable to many of the other lies Satan wants us to believe.

Norma was one of the most placating individuals I had ever met. She had been physically and emotionally battered as a child and had grown up to be an extremely docile adult. Much like a puppy rolls over to expose its tummy to an aggressor, Norma had adopted an unconscious strategy of acting helpless in order to ward off criticism and punishment. Her countenance and body language constantly broadcast the question, "How can you kick me when I'm down?" Her entire life was dominated by her need to prove to everyone that she meant no harm.

As a child, Norma had learned that people would place fewer demands on her and come to her aid if she acted helpless. The disadvantage of playing the helpless role, however, was that others continued to victimize her. Whenever anyone became aggressive or demanding, Norma became psychologically immobilized. Consequently, she had been the victim of ongoing emotional and physical abuse well into her adulthood.

Yet, because of her early training, Norma continued to believe that her codependent behavior was essential to her safety. Some may find it impossible to understand how she could believe that the very behavior that resulted in her continued victimization was her perceived pathway to safety and security. But for thousands of people caught in the trap of codependency, it's no mystery. Such a distortion simply validates the fact that Satan can use the abuse or neglect we suffer as children to convince us of illogical, irrational beliefs.

FACING OUR NEED FOR CONTROL

While many exhibit their codependency by being "bossy" or willful, as Harry did, there are just as many helpless codependents like Norma. *Control* is always the issue. Our misperceptions, combined with the numbing of our heart, cause us to renounce our responsibility to make choices for ourselves.

We must admit and deal with three areas if we are to get beyond our need to be in control. *The first is that we are angry.* We act out our anger either by being bossy (not letting anything go wrong) or by being helpless (not letting anything go right). Both of these behaviors are dishonest.

Second, we feel entitled to all the things and experiences we never had as children. Feeling entitled often means that we take without asking and feel cheated when things don't go our way. We need to give up our conviction that we have been cheated. Relying on the fact that God is sovereign and nothing that ever happened to us was out of his control, we can choose to let God determine the course of our lives. He alone knows what we need and what will bring us to a point where we can genuinely reflect the character of his Son, Jesus Christ. We need to be willing to see even the bad times as a part of his plan. Those times will be used by God to our advantage—we simply need to wait on him.

Third, we are ashamed. We don't believe that we can afford to let people see us as we really are. Typically, we either present an image of who we think we should be or of who we believe the other person wishes us to be. Among other bad effects, this dishonesty contributes to a lack of *boundaries*—those invisible parameters that allow us the freedom to be individuals.

Personal boundaries define where we end and others begin. They allow us to differ from others, to have likes and dislikes, to decide not to "go with the flow" when we are surrounded by people who may be behaving in a way that we regard as "unChristian" or ungodly. Boundaries allow us to define what we expect from others and what we feel we can give to others without damaging ourselves. They help us to have an understanding of what is "our stuff" and what belongs to someone else.

For instance, suppose we do something that insults or annoys someone. Personal boundaries help us to determine whether our behavior was truly insulting or annoying, or whether their negative reaction is because of some event in their past about which we knew nothing. We may still choose to apologize because the other person was hurt, but we know that their pain did not originate with us. When someone shares their emotional pain with us, good boundaries allow us to empathize with that person without taking their pain onto ourselves as if it were our own. We know what's "theirs" and what's "ours."

When our boundaries are intact, we know when we are happy or unhappy. Without appropriate boundaries, we can't always be sure. Good boundaries allow us to be aware of the circumstances around us without their determining our mood. We trust our intuition. We are accountable for our behavior and hold others accountable for theirs.

Intact boundaries help us to know our limits, to know what we need in order to maintain our physical, emotional, and spiritual health. And they allow us to make allowances for those needs without feeling guilty. Boundaries provide the self-assurance to say no when someone asks too much of us. Perhaps what they're asking will simply be the straw that breaks the camel's back on a day that is already too full of activity. Perhaps their demands will violate our body and spirit. Children who have suffered the violation of sexual abuse, for instance, have had their boundaries smashed. This leaves them vulnerable to further molestation because they lack the confidence to refuse the next time someone demands too much of them.

Spiritual boundaries serve a similar function. They allow us to determine what we can expect from God. Spiritual truths can set us free from the belief that we are just "worms" who deserve nothing from God. If Christ had not died for our sins, we would deserve nothing from God. But as his adopted children, we have the "right" to expect our Daddy-God to act toward us in the ways he has promised he would.

Spiritual boundaries based in truth are important to us as Christians. They help us to define who we are in Christ. They provide us the self-assurance to say no to violation in the spiritual domain. When our spiritual boundaries have been violated, we will exhibit some signs of that violation. We are not sure whether we can count on God and feel that we must always be proving our worth to him. We take as truth the most recent doctrinal opinion we've heard because we aren't really sure what we believe. We don't feel qualified or worthy to rightfully discern evil.

We may feel hurt and victimized but never feel angry about it. We may feel afraid or confused much of the time, unsure about where self-preservation ends and selfishness begins. Since "good soldiers never complain," we don't feel we deserve to express our own needs. We tend to accept our "lot in life," no matter how dismal, rather than seek God for ways to change or improve it. We may see others as causing our excitement or having the power to "make" us happy or satisfied. We're always seeking that "mountain top" experience because we don't know how to achieve spiritual joy and contentment ourselves.

We see everyone as more powerful than we are and act out of compliance or compromise to the "shoulds." We don't know how to meet the needs of others without giving ourselves away, keeping nothing for ourselves or our families. We live to please others while secretly resenting the fact that we always seem to be the one doing the giving. We can't conceive of ourselves as having worth outside of our ability to perform on someone else's behalf. We assume that "going the extra mile" means that we don't have the right to say

"Enough!"—even when we're done in, burned out, and dying on the vine.

We may be obsessed with others or their behavior toward us. We feel we prove our love for others only when we give so much it hurts. We confess all of our shortcomings to anyone who will listen, rather than seeking one or two trustworthy people to whom we can choose to be accountable. We constantly make excuses for others' obnoxiousness. We take on others' problems.

We aren't sure we are entitled to time alone or with our families. We may be constantly seeking relationships with people who are too busy to notice us. We aren't sure whether our hunger for fellowship with others is "acceptable." After all, isn't God supposed to meet all of our needs?

Do any of these beliefs sound familiar? When Satan smashes our spiritual boundaries by causing us to believe his lies, he can count on us to continue to victimize ourselves as a result. And he is able to trick us into believing that the members of our Christian community are the culprits—and sometimes they are.

Believing lies about who we are and what God expects of us sets us up for all sorts of complications in our Christian lives. We live with fear, anger, hurt, and bitterness because "others" demand too much of us. Soon it appears that life "in the Spirit" is no different than life was in the world. We simply don't know we have the right to say no when we need to.

We may also develop anger and bitterness because we don't know we have the right to say "ouch" when someone hurts us. We believe that "turning the other cheek" means lying down and printing "WELCOME" on our backs. At the core of our despair is the belief that God's Word holds no power for us.

Jesus' confrontation with Satan in the desert demonstrated the way to set spiritual boundaries (see Mt 4:1-11). He spoke out God's truth, and we must do the same. Satan can only violate us spiritually by convincing us of his lies. When we know the truth, we no longer believe him. Saying the truth out loud forces our adversary to listen.

Over time we will begin to notice that the things that were once difficult for us no longer are. We will begin to see the benefit of having boundaries and have the knowledge and confidence to tell Satan and his demons to go back where they belong. Some of the most commonly violated spiritual boundaries are related to the following areas.

Our freedom in Christ. We may end up feeling as if we are not "good" Christians unless we give up everything we enjoy. I have known many who have given up everything from reading science fiction to attending baseball games because they believed they were not supposed to enjoy themselves once they were Christians. Scripture says that everything is permissible, but not everything is beneficial (see 1 Cor 6:12; 10:23).

God's grace. Many of us believe that grace is for others, but *we* have to earn our place in God's family. We begin to set up rules that we must follow, like reading the Bible and praying for so many minutes or hours each day. Or we believe that we must attend church so many times each week. In reality, as our relationship with God deepens we will *choose* to spend time with the Lord in prayer and study of his Word. Being in God's presence is a privilege, not a duty. His grace is sufficient (see 2 Cor 12:9).

Faith versus works. I suspect that all of us have been told—either overtly or covertly—how much of our time or money we need to give to God's work in order to make it to heaven, or what other duties we must perform in order to do so. We may even have asked someone else to tell us what to do. But we are justified by faith, not by works (see Rom 4:5; 4:13; 5:1-2; 9:30).

The consequences of our sin. When we feel guilty over something for which we have already repented, we can be sure that Satan is attempting to violate our boundaries. We are not rewarded according to our iniquity (see Ps 103:10).

The time it takes to heal. We may believe that we need to simply "snap out of it." If only we were "good" Christians, we would already be healed and our recovery process would be complete the moment we became a member of God's family. The truth is, no one—including us—can determine God's plans and timetable for our lives (see Jer 29:11-14; Phil 1:6).

Expressing negative feelings. We may be horrified to admit that we are angry with God. We may be afraid to ask God some of our hard questions like, "Where were you when this happened to me?" But God accepts our negative emotions as readily as our positive ones (see Jb 13; Eph 4:26).

RELEASE FROM SLAVERY

If there is an ounce of life left in the codependent, he or she will fight to gain and keep control. It is simply "the nature of the beast." Our hearts are fallow and need to be turned over with divine love that is experienced and not just read about or observed. That maniacal need for control is the fallow ground. We must accept the challenge to move over and allow God to take control.

To most of us, leaving our codependent behavior behind causes us to feel like the Israelites did upon leaving Egypt. I don't doubt that the Israelites would have turned around and marched back to Egypt if God had truly given them that option. But our heavenly Father is more loving than that. He doesn't give in to our temper tantrums or our insistence that we are better off in bondage. God commits himself to our release in order to help us gain the freedom he created us to enjoy—even if it means prying our fingers off of the very thing we don't want to relinquish, one finger at a time.

The Israelites wandered in the desert for forty years. Fortunately, we don't have to spend that kind of time leaving our personal "Egypt" behind. I believe that Twelve Step programs make available to us a proven path through the desert of our addictions or compulsions. This process of spiritual recovery has helped thousands of slaves to be released from their bondage—whether it be to drugs, alcohol, overeating, compulsive gambling, overspending, or sexual addictions. The same Twelve Step process has proven useful in overcoming codependency issues as well.

I would caution the reader, however, that this program of recovery depends on a *group process.* Recovery doesn't happen in a vacuum. Such programs are almost everywhere these days. You need not go it alone. Since the Twelve Steps are commonly available to all, I will not take the time here to review the steps in depth. I simply want the reader to know that a route of escape is accessible and has stood the test of time.

The Twelve Steps

1. We admitted we were powerless over alcohol—that our lives had become unmanageable.
2. Came to believe that a Power greater than ourselves could restore us to sanity.
3. Made a decision to turn our will and our lives over to the care of God *as we understood Him.*
4. Made a searching and fearless moral inventory of ourselves.
5. Admitted to God, to ourselves, and to another human being the exact nature of our wrongs.
6. Were entirely ready to have God remove all these defects of character.
7. Humbly asked Him to remove our shortcomings.
8. Made a list of all persons we had harmed, and became willing to make amends to them all.
9. Made direct amends to such people wherever possible, except when to do so would injure them or others.
10. Continued to take personal inventory and when we were wrong promptly admitted it.
11. Sought through prayer and meditation to improve our conscious contact with God, *as we understood Him,* praying only for knowledge of His will for us and the power to carry that out.
12. Having had a spiritual awakening as the result of these

steps, we tried to carry this message to alcoholics, and to practice these principles in all our affairs.*

*The Twelve Steps are reprinted with permission of Alcoholics Anonymous World Services, Inc. Permission to reprint and adapt the Twelve Steps does not mean that A.A. has reviewed or approved the contents of this publication, nor that A.A. agrees with the views expressed herein. A.A. is a program of recovery from alcoholism—use of the Twelve Steps in connection with programs and activities which are patterned after A.A., but which address other problems, does not imply otherwise.

JESUS IS THE TRUTH

Jesus relinquished his life on the cross so that Satan would no longer be able to blind us to the truth about God's love for us. Jesus said, "I am the way and the truth and the life. No one comes to the Father except through me" (Jn 14:6). Scripture also refers to the Holy Spirit as "the Comforter" who "will guide you into all truth" (Jn 16:13). It is not possible for us to have truth in our lives without Jesus. If you don't already have Jesus in your life, I would like to invite you to consider your need for him.

All of Satan's lies can be exposed by the light of God's truth. All we need to do is accept Jesus Christ as our Lord and Savior. Then we will no longer need to pretend that we can "go it alone." If that thought brings you reassurance, then let me encourage you to say this prayer from your heart so that you may have a relationship with Jesus Christ and come to know his truth, making it your own for all of eternity.

Heavenly Father, I don't want to be fooled by Satan's lies any longer. I recognize that your Son, Jesus, died for me on the cross and that the truth about your love was demonstrated through his life, death, and resurrection. I ask you to forgive all my sins. Jesus, I ask you to come into my heart and pray that you would make your truth known to me as you promised. Holy Spirit, be with me and fill me, I pray in Jesus' name. Amen.

When you have God's truth in your life, Satan's lies no longer have power over you. You have become a son or daughter of God. "Because you are sons, God sent the Spirit of his Son into our hearts, the Spirit who calls out, 'Abba, Father.' So you are no longer a slave, but a son; and since you are a son, God has made you also an heir" (Gal 4:6-7).

A Practical Exercise
✦ ✦ ✦

Study this list of Satan's common lies and place a check by those you think you may have believed as the result of your abuse or neglect. Ask God to help you spot them each time they come up in your thought patterns from now on. Speak the appropriate truths out loud. Declare, in Jesus' name, that you are not going to believe Satan's lies anymore.

1. *Satan's lie*: God can't love me.
   God's truth: "All the ways of the LORD are loving" (Ps 25:10); "The LORD is... loving toward all he has made" (Ps 145:13).
2. *Satan's lie*: I am worthless.
   God's truth: "Your body is a temple of the Holy Spirit, who is in you... you were bought at a price" (1 Cor 6:19-20).
3. *Satan's lie*: Sin will always get the better of me.
   God's truth: "No, in all these things we are more than conquerors through him who loved us" (Rom 8:37).
4. *Satan's lie*: God can't be trusted.
   God's truth: "The LORD is good, a refuge in times of trouble. He cares for those who trust in him,..." (Na 1:7).
5. *Satan's lie*: I don't need God.
   God's truth: "Do not hold against us the sins of the fathers; may your mercy come quickly to meet us, for we are in desperate need" (Ps 79:8).

6. *Satan's lie:* God will always keep me guessing.

    God's truth: "Trust in the LORD with all your heart and lean not on your own understanding; in all your ways acknowledge him, and he will make your paths straight" (Prv 3:5-6).

7. *Satan's lie:* Sin and darkness offers relief, while righteous ness demands impossible perfection.

    God's truth: "Everyone who sins is a slave to sin" (Jn 8:34); "The wages of sin is death" (Rom 6:23); "The LORD rewards every man for his righteousness" (1 Sm 26:23); "The fruit of righteousness will be peace" (Is 32:17).

8. *Satan's lie:* God's secret purpose is to punish me.

    God's truth: "Delight yourself in the LORD and he will give you the desires of your heart" (Ps 37:4); "He is patient with you, not wanting anyone to perish" (2 Pt 3:9); "'I know the plans I have for you,' declares the LORD, 'plans to prosper you and not to harm you, plans to give you hope and a future'" (Jer 29:11).

9. *Satan's lie:* God expects me to be something I can't be.

    God's truth: "For it is by grace you have been saved, through faith—and this not from yourselves, it is the gift of God" (Eph 2:8).

10. *Satan's lie:* God isn't interested in my comfort. He only wants people who are willing to sacrifice themselves.

    God's truth: "For I desire mercy, not sacrifice, and acknowledgment of God rather than burnt offerings" (Hos 6:6); "The work of God is this: to believe in the one he has sent" (Jn 6:29).

TEN

Who Is the Inner Child?

*For he chose us in him before the creation of the world to be holy
and blameless in his sight. In love he predestined us to be adopted
as his sons through Jesus Christ, in accordance with his pleasure
and will—to the praise of his glorious grace, which he has freely
given us in the One he loves.* **Ephesians 1:4-6**

T HE CONCEPT OF THE INNER CHILD has gained immense
popularity within the psychological community in recent years. The term has become familiar to most people
who are seeking recovery from childhood abuse and neglect.

But the popularity of any new idea carries with it risks of
misuse as well. The concept of the inner child is no exception. In some circles the inner child has become almost mys-
tical—as if there really is a separate little person dwelling
within one's mind. Embracing the concept in those terms,
however, presents an inherent danger.

Peggy was a forty-year-old woman who had endured extreme abuse as a child. She had begun to recover repressed
memories of incest within her family about a year and a half
before she came to see me for counseling, and had become
acquainted with the concept of the inner child through her
participation in incest survivors' support groups during that
time. Peggy collected a smattering of information about the

inner child, but hesitated to embrace the concept at first—despite the fact that her friends claimed it was "the only effective way" to deal with incest recovery.

Eventually Peggy's emotional pain made her willing to try anything. She began to search for her child within. Having no real guidance—and certainly no Christian guidance—she eventually "found" numerous "children within." In fact, she found fourteen in all and had assigned them names and personality traits before she realized that she was in serious trouble. She had come to see herself as thoroughly fragmented.

More than one of her therapist friends suggested to her the likelihood that she was a "multiple personality." Given the severity of the abuse she had suffered as a child, that theory seemed plausible. Peggy was terribly concerned. She realized that the more "children/personalities" she identified, the more fragmented and out of control she felt. Peggy could see that she was losing ground rather than gaining it as she continued to work with these "inner children."

The construct we call "the inner child" is simply a metaphor that helps us to create a mental picture of the child we once were. It provides us with a way to acknowledge the emotions we were afraid to express when we originally suffered traumatic events. This concept also helps us to begin to see the child we were as defenseless and undeserving of mistreatment. "The inner child" is not an actual being with a separate identity that lurks in our minds.

Eventually, with the help of some knowledgeable Christians, Peggy began to understand the truth about "the inner child" and could see how she had gone astray. She reclaimed all the parts of herself that she had separated. Using the three-step process explained in chapter four (1. Define the lie's content and the spirit maintaining the lie; 2. Separate oneself from the spirit's influence through repentance and by binding the spirit; 3. Refute the lie with truth from Scripture.), Peggy also obtained release from the negative spiritual forces that had taken advantage of her confusion.

Peggy made quick progress after that. But she tended to speak about staying "in touch with her emotions" rather than "in touch with her inner child" from then on. For her the concept of the inner child had become a stumbling block. For most of us, it can be a useful and welcome tool.

EMOTIONS NOT MEMORIES

As children, our minds may not perceive and process data correctly, but our hearts are already fulfilling their purpose. Our hearts are the spring from which all our emotions flow. Very young children have no difficulty expressing their grief and anger as adults so often do. But growing up in an abusive atmosphere causes us to detach from our feelings—to silence our hearts.

We are taught—either overtly or covertly—that expressing our emotions is unacceptable. Our feelings are invalidated at every turn. Consequently, getting back in touch with our long suppressed emotions is a major therapeutic hurdle. Our thought-life and the symptoms we exhibit may tell us that we have buried memories, but healing can only take place when we reconnect with our long buried emotions.

Until children reach the age of twelve or thirteen, they are developmentally incapable of making sound judgments about the world because they base their understanding of events on something called "egocentrism." From the child's point of view, the world revolves around him or her. The child sees him or herself as the cause of everything that happens to one—including abuse. Added to that is the simplistic moral reasoning that "bad things happen to bad people." It is easy to see why those of us who suffered abuse in childhood have such low self-esteem and why we have stopped listening to our hearts.

If the trauma is sufficient, the child may also suffer a developmental arrest. The child's capacity to process data about the world becomes stunted. He or she will continue—even

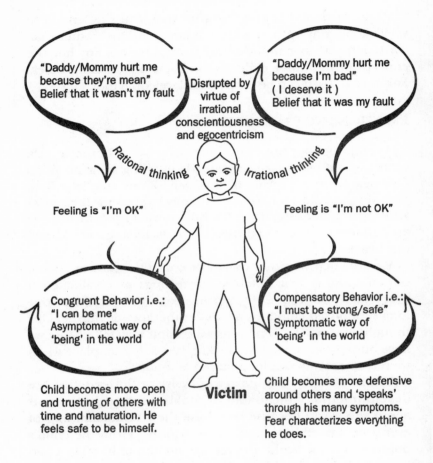

into adulthood—to process information at the level of maturity achieved when the abuse took place. Many survivors continue to feel that everything that goes wrong is somehow their fault.

If children try to come to terms with what their victimization indicates about their worth as a person before they reach the age of twelve or thirteen, they will undoubtedly draw the wrong conclusions. The Victim's Creed in chapter two gives a good many examples of the wrong conclusions most of us have carried into adulthood.

Adults are frequently unaware of a specific trauma that took place in their childhood, or they may be in denial about how truly painful it was. Because of this dynamic, it is often helpful to allow the adult to become an "observer" while expressing the intense feelings that have remained so long buried.

That is where the concept of the inner child can be helpful. It allows us to assign those intense emotions to the child we were, while leaving the adult we are free to reassess the child's experiences. In other words, the concept of the inner child is simply a therapeutic tool. It is a means of viewing our past from a different angle, making it possible for us to modify our belief system.

Sometimes we are unable to describe childhood abuse with any degree of certainty. With the use of the inner child, we can sometimes paint an accurate representation of our childhood on the canvas of our imagination. This enables us to pursue recovery from childhood abuse even when our memories are not very specific. Recovery does not necessarily require concrete memories. But the recovery of our repressed emotions is essential.

Through the use of imagery, the typical "talking cure" of the therapist can be exchanged for visualization. With this tool, we can tap into the reservoir of feelings and attending memories that might otherwise remain repressed. Vivid reminders of our past may come to mind as we begin to sort through our memories in much the same way we might sort through old photographs. We will find it easier to recall the dilemma we experienced as children, simply because we have given ourselves permission to do so.

In the process of imagining our inner child, it becomes easier for our adult minds to relinquish the tendency to criticize or censure the feelings that these images bring back to us. When we allow our feelings to be reawakened in response to our mental images, we find that we can abandon many of the psychic defenses we have constructed around memories of traumatic events. The concept of the inner child enables us to see ourselves as children—perhaps for the first time. We no longer view ourselves as the "miniature adults" we often believed we were as children.

While this may seem like "slight of hand," there is nothing magical about imagery. In fact, it has been a useful method in the treatment of cancer patients. Imagery has often been able to help patients overcome inoperable forms of the disease. Research suggests that the human mind has a God-given capacity to combat illness through imagery.

ONE PICTURE IS BETTER THAN A THOUSAND WORDS

Sherry entered counseling because she was having difficulty coping with life in general. The behaviors she described to me indicated that she had suffered abuse or neglect as a child. I explained the concept of the inner child to Sherry and asked her to picture what her inner child might look like.

Sherry described a Dickens-type waif completely alone in the shed near the house she had lived in as a youngster. Then feelings of being trapped began to surface for her. She noticed that her imagination added that there was no door knob on the shed door and the door was stuck tight. She could not get out. This was her heart's dreary impression of her past.

The concept of the inner child allowed Sherry's unconscious to reveal the essence of the truth about her past in a way that seemed less threatening than the recovery of actual memories might have been. I believe that the mind's ability to create such images reflects the fact that God has designed the human spirit to bear witness to the cry of our hearts.

Sherry and I prayed together at every session that God would sanctify her imagination and reveal to her only that which was true. As she talked about the child trapped in the shed, Sherry experienced the fear and loneliness she had known. She could see that she had, indeed, felt those emotions all those years ago, despite the fact that she was not yet able to recall her circumstances.

I also asked Sherry to keep a journal of her dreams. As

hidden trauma begins to surface, I have found dream work to be very productive. Sherry and I recognized that God interprets all dreams (see Gn 40:8), so we prayed for God's interpretation of her dreams. In this way, her nights became as productive as her days in her journey toward healing.

Dark and scary assailants chased Sherry in her dreams. Her only friend was a clown in a red suit. This comic figure visited her regularly and seemed to protect her as she huddled at his feet. After prayer, Sherry came to the conclusion that the clown represented the comedic way in which she had learned to cope with her pain. She had attempted to hide her pain and loneliness and win her parents' love by entertaining others and by maintaining a facade of cheerfulness.

Eventually Sherry began to regain more of her memories. Because she had proven to herself that it was safe now to acknowledge and express some of the pain she had previously denied, her unconscious was finally able to reveal the memories it had kept hidden for so long.

Sherry remembered her mother's harshness. She recalled being forced to sit in her darkened bedroom for hours in punishment for her misdeeds, awaiting Mother's switch. This explained her impression of having been trapped. She realized that both of her parents had ridiculed her childlike spontaneity and had emotionally and verbally battered her. She had, in fact, escaped to the shed near her house to be alone. Sherry could see clearly now what a bind she had been in as a child. She was completely dependent on her parents as her caretakers. She needed their love and affection as well as their material provision. Only the latter had been available to her.

As children, we convince ourselves that we have power over our circumstances by telling ourselves this lie: *if we are unloved, then we must be unlovable.* If that is the case, then we still have control over the outcome. All we have to do is *make* ourselves lovable. Hope remains alive. We can continue to cling to the belief that we may finally find a way to make Mommy and Daddy love us. When that love is not forthcoming, however, the conclusion remains: "If I'm unloved I must be unlovable."

As we view childhood events through adult eyes, we see that we were vulnerable, in need of loving discipline and nurturance, and that the abuse we endured was a reflection of someone else's deficits rather than our own. The concept of the inner child enables us to access feelings and memories that might otherwise stay repressed.

What if our imaginations "run away" with us and we "remember" things that didn't really happen? Providing we are aware that what we imagine may not be based in "reality," this usually is not a problem. Suppose a little boy lives next door to someone who owns a ferocious-looking bull dog. The child may believe that neighbor is "mean" for owning a dog that frightens him. The neighbor may actually be a perfectly wonderful human being. But, the child's emotional response can be at the root of a trauma that needs to be processed— whether his perception of the neighbor as a "meanie" is accurate or not.

In this case, our imaginations may supply us with images of the "mean" neighbor because that is what we *perceived* to be the cause of our trauma. It is the *emotions caused by the trauma* that we are really interested in processing. And for such a purpose, this sort of imagery serves nicely.

RE-PARENTING

All humans need to be nurtured through touch. As a result, those of us who were physically or sexually abused suffer a double bind as we strive to recover. Some of us never experienced a nurturing touch. For us, physical contact was often the stuff of nightmares. We suffer what is often referred to as "skin hunger," yet we associate touch with abuse. We long for the comfort and validation touch can provide, but shrink from it when it's offered. Many of us cause havoc in our relationships because we send a double message to our partners: "touch me/get away."

Inner child work can allow us to see God as our parent. We

can begin to see what God says to us and allows to happen in our lives as his "re-parenting." We begin to watch as he meets our needs, rather than waiting for "somebody" to sense our need and meet it for us.

Part of that re-parenting process can include overcoming our fear of touch. We can use something like a doll or a stuffed animal or a favorite pillow to create the impression of being held and touched. I encourage my clients to hold the chosen object close—with their eyes closed—and imagine that God is holding them in the same way. They can remember God's loving words from Scripture while they have their eyes closed.

This sort of exercise is usually terribly uncomfortable at first. But with practice it becomes easier. With persistence all of us can overcome the discomfort—the feelings of foolishness—and begin to see ourselves as deserving of that sort of loving "parenting." Our defenses will begin to soften. Eventually, touch is no longer threatening to us.

Naturally, we need to avoid the current trend to turn inner child work into an excuse for self-absorption. We need always to keep this kind of tool in its proper place. Something like the "inner child" can become an idol in our lives—just as food, money, alcohol, or any number of other things can become idols.

Nor is our inner child meant to provide an excuse for poor behavior. The concept of the inner child isn't meant to allow us to throw public temper tantrums and then dismiss them as "simply my inner child giving voice to his/her feelings." Such behavior is no more excusable in the name of an inner child than in any adult. As Christians we need to use discipline in dealing with the emotions of "our inner child," just as we would with our flesh and blood children.

Providing we do not use inner child work as an excuse for self-absorption or poor behavior, this therapeutic tool almost always proves to be a wonderful boon to the person recovering from childhood trauma. Inner child work often helps to expose some of the lies we came to believe as children.

Once we have wholeheartedly embraced the loving things that God says to us in his Word, Satan can be rendered powerless to intrude upon us with his deadly accusations. We learn to dismiss our critical self-talk which has become judge and jury. Satan is no longer free to insist on the maximum sentence in the courtroom of our minds.

At this point a support group can be very helpful. Group members can meet our need for human touch in a non-threatening atmosphere. Our need for skin contact must be met in a safe, non-seductive way. A loving embrace given in Christ-like love can be the catalyst for a life-changing breakthrough. I have seen it happen countless times.

We can't expect to act differently simply because we wish to or because we're trying harder. We must be shown *how* to act differently. We share the same failing that the apostle Paul noted: "For I know that in me (that is, in my flesh) nothing good dwells; for to will is present with me, but *how* to perform what is good I do not find" (Rom 7:18 NKJV).

We need to learn how to relate effectively in a family atmosphere. A recovery group can help us learn to cope with family issues and family dynamics by being our surrogate family. We can explore ways to become *interdependent* rather than *codependent* with our "family" members. A group composed of brothers and sisters in Christ—one with Christian facilitators—is particularly effective. As Christians, we are already family. The members of such a group possess a high level of commitment to one another as a result.

The "group process" affords us an opportunity to watch as others model appropriate behavior for us. In that way we can learn how to act appropriately. We need a place to practice our new ways of relating. In a group setting we can find encouragement. We can finally hear the loving words we longed to hear as children. Group members can validate our emotional responses for the first time in our lives.

Inner child work is meant to last only for a season in our lives. Eventually we will learn to reconnect with our emotions without needing to attribute them to the child we once were. It is a great accomplishment when we begin to listen to our hearts once again.

We can begin to see as liabilities the defenses we originally built in order to protect ourselves. We will discover that our defenses have walled us off from intimacy with others, with ourselves, and with God. We can begin the scary but rewarding process of disassembling those walls brick by brick. In time and with patience, we will step out into the light of Christ.

A Practical Exercise
✦ ✦ ✦

1. Search the Scriptures for verses in which God tells us how much he loves us. Here are just a few to get you started: Jeremiah 31:3; Romans 8:35-39; Ephesians 2:4 and 3:16-19; and 2 Thessalonians 2:16.

2. Memorize as many of these verses as you can.

3. Say one or more of the verses you have memorized out loud whenever you hear yourself thinking or saying negative things about yourself. While looking at a photograph of yourself as a child, direct a spiritual blessing toward the child you were. Then pray this prayer:

> *Lord, right now I declare that [say whatever negative thing you've been telling yourself] is a lie. I command Satan, who is the Father of lies, to depart from me with all of his demons, in the name of the Lord Jesus Christ.*
>
> *Lord, your Word says [repeat the Scripture verse that applies]. I believe your Word is truth. You have made me your son/daughter. I am your child, and Satan has no right to accuse me. I accept, with thanksgiving, the grace in which I stand by virtue of Christ's shed blood. Amen.*

ELEVEN

Anger: The Path to Forgiveness

"In your anger do not sin": Do not let the sun go down while you are still angry, and do not give the devil a foothold. **Ephesians 4:26-27**

ANDY WAS A THIRTY-FIVE-YEAR-OLD executive with four children who came to me for help because his excessive jealousy was ruining his marriage. He admitted feeling foolish about his obsession with his wife's faithfulness. She had never given him any reason to be concerned about her fidelity. Yet Andy complained that he just didn't seem to be able to stop it. His relationship with his wife had been so adversely affected by his constant suspicion that they barely spoke anymore, except to fight.

Andy described his childhood as "okay," but spoke about that time completely without emotion. It was as if his past belonged to someone else. Over a period of many weeks, however, he constructed a picture for me of a very unhappy little boy. Andy's mother had divorced his father when he was six years old. Shortly afterward she discovered that she couldn't survive financially on her own, so the two of them moved in with Andy's grandmother. Soon his mother became completely preoccupied with her job and her social life—a distant, unreachable figure who had no time to spend with a "useless" little boy. He was left to his grandmother's care.

His mother remarried when Andy was ten. He moved into a new house with his mother and stepfather. The boy thought then that they would finally be a family and hoped that he would finally receive from his mother the attention he craved. But Mom wanted time for herself now that things were different. And she wanted time to spend with her new husband. Andy continued to be "farmed out" to his grandmother whenever his presence was inconvenient.

Andy didn't feel that it was "right" to be angry about the way he grew up. His grandmother had given him everything he needed, hadn't she? He told himself that there were lots of kids who grew up without even a grandmother to love them. So what did he have to complain about? He stuffed his anger and hurt down inside year after year.

When Andy began dating, he discovered that he preferred the company of passive women—women who were willing to endure his possessiveness and extreme jealousy. He was driven nearly insane by his constant conviction that any woman he was involved with was about to leave him. One relationship after another ended in an ugly confrontation when his current "love" decided she'd had enough. Andy finally married, but now his marriage was about to blow up in his face. He was desperate for some answers.

Andy's jealousy revealed an immense need to control anyone he loved in a frantic attempt to keep them from abandoning him as he felt his mother had. Andy and I began to work on "finding" his true emotions stemming from his mother's emotional abandonment. He needed to get to "the heart of the matter."

I explained to Andy that his controlling strategies were designed to keep underlying feelings safely hidden. Feeling "original pain" once more seemed too risky. Andy could see that unless he dealt with his original pain, he would continue to employ defensive strategies in his current relationships which would simply keep him stuck in an addictive style of relating to the world. That addiction meant returning time and again to old behaviors designed to ward off any feelings of true vulnerability.

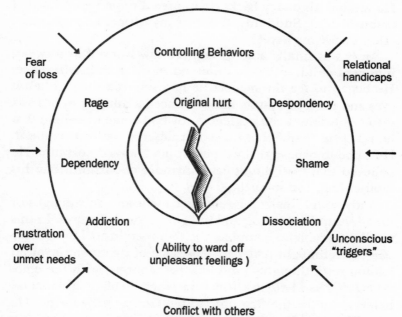

Key: Any experience/situation that parallels or approaches original hurt must be warded off by controlling behavior.

A FOUR-STEP PROCESS OF HEALING

Like so many survivors of abuse and neglect, Andy needed to go through a four-step process: regression, revision, resolution, and reconciliation. To begin the first step of *regression*, I asked him to think back to certain scenes from his childhood. I wanted to help him begin to see and feel, once again, the pain he had tried so hard to bury. Andy needed to begin to own his feelings again. Our first efforts failed but we kept at it.

One day, I asked Andy to picture himself on his grandmother's front porch watching his mother drive away. As he visualized her car getting further and further away, he realized he didn't want to be there. He wanted to be at home. He wanted his daddy back. He wanted a mommy who would listen to him. Suddenly, there in my office, he screamed, "Don't leave me here!"

Andy was finally able to cry. He saw himself as a sweet, innocent child, one who deserved more than indifference. He began to see the neglect he had suffered through adult eyes and realized that he had embraced a number of lies as a result of his mother's neglect. Andy had come to believe that he must be "bad," that he didn't deserve better treatment. He came to believe that women would always desert him. He believed that God didn't care anymore about him than his mother had, and so forth.

Andy could finally reassess his conclusions in the light of his adult understanding and in light of the Scriptures. In this way, he was able to complete the therapeutic goal of the *revision* of his thought patterns. This stage of treatment involved joining right thoughts (and new perceptions) with the emotions Andy had held in check for so long. Feeling understood helped him for the first time to see God as truly loving. He felt affirmed in his spirit.

In order to help Andy enter the *resolution* phase of his recovery, I explained the grief process as described by Kübler-Ross. The stages of grief are: shock, denial, anger, despair and mourning, and acceptance. Andy needed to complete that process if he was ever to attain resolution.

In the following sessions, I asked him to stand before an empty chair that represented his mother's absence. Using a foam-covered bat, he hit the seat of a chair or a couch cushion, allowing himself to vent the anger that had existed in his heart all along. As he hit the chair, blow upon blow, he voiced his conviction that he had deserved more than his mother's indifference.

Andy learned to admit his vulnerability once again. He

learned to speak honestly about his feelings and fears. He learned to face his pain and to grieve for the child within him. This simply becomes another way of embracing the truth and turning away from a lie. We needn't hide our anger in order to earn God's love. God loves us, just as we are—even when we are angry. And, in fact, God is angry on our behalf whenever the forces of darkness cause us to suffer abuse or neglect.

Eventually Andy was able to talk openly with his wife about his fears rather than acting jealous and controlling. He didn't need to control his wife anymore because the pain of rejection was no longer unfinished business from his past. His marriage began to heal.

Reconciliation came about in one of Andy's final sessions as he faced that same empty chair and voiced, aloud, his forgiveness for his mother. In that act of forgiveness, he also released himself from the bitterness that had held him prisoner for so many years. Andy needed to be reconciled with himself, as well. He needed to reclaim the parts of himself that he had buried because he had deemed them unacceptable, and give all of himself to God.

Andy also became reconciled with God. He learned that, while God is always fair, life is not. As a result of giving voice to his anger, Andy saw that God didn't "strike him dead." God continued to love him and beckon to him as a loving Father. He realized that being angry for a little while was all right because it represented the truth about the feelings he had hidden as a child. They were very real feelings in response to very real pain. Unspoken anger produces a root of bitterness. Freedom to express that anger within the safety of God's grace provides opportunity for an emotional release that can be life-changing.

Andy realized that God did care and that he could really trust him. God had always cared and had grieved along with him. As Andy acknowledged and vented his anger, hatred, and bitterness, the defenses he no longer needed began to crumble. His excessive jealousy diminished. His chronic despair was replaced by genuine grieving. Gradually, God turned Andy's mourning into dancing.

SETTLING FOR POWER

As children we cried out for the assurance that we mattered to someone. But, when it became apparent to us that we had no significance to those who were most important to us, we learned to cover our hurt by convincing ourselves that we could live very nicely without those people. We claimed *power* in place of *significance.*

We derived power from denying our emotions—struggling to remain unflappable, striving to have all our own answers. We learned to live out our lives strictly in our heads rather than our hearts. We often denied our feelings because our caretakers interpreted any show of emotion as a challenge to their authority or as an intentional reminder of their failures. In Andy's case, no one was there to notice his feelings anyway, so what was the use?

We also denied our feelings because our anger or sorrow reminded us that we were at the mercy of the adults who abused or neglected us. That didn't feel safe. We convinced ourselves of a kind of "omnipotence" in order to feel less threatened. And many of us find it necessary to deny our memories in order to keep our sense of power intact.

In addition, our abusers often led us to believe that we were responsible for much of what went on around us. We were often "parentified" through having been enlisted by the adults in our lives as sexual partners, confidants, and "helpers." Playing these roles added to our feelings of omnipotence. We became hungry for any knowledge that would help us show the world we were capable. We were driven to become "do it alls" and "know it alls."

Satan's trick all the while is the same as it was in the garden. He comes along and offers the thought that eating from the Tree of Knowledge will make us self-sufficient. Having the answers to our problems will keep us safe. All we have to do is attend more seminars, read more books, or become therapy junkies.

In order to recover from the abuse and neglect we suffered as children, we have to renounce the false power we have claimed. We need to eat from the Tree of Life and give up our self-sufficiency. We need to acknowledge, absolutely, that God alone is omnipotent. Only then will we feel safe enough to unlock the secret compartment of our hearts and truly feel all of our emotions—especially our anger.

Repressed anger is continually recycled within us. It plays itself out in our decisions and reactions to others over and over again, becoming progressively more toxic. Even when we have no consciousness of our anger, it relentlessly continues to poison us. Repressed anger will remain a poison within until we express it.

In addition to that very excellent reason for "finding" and expressing our anger, God's Word tells us that we must forgive. But true forgiveness can only follow anger. What is there to forgive if we have nothing to be angry about? When we choose to "forget" what has happened to us before we have fully expressed our anger, we are simply choosing to maintain our control—our omnipotence.

Denying the pain of our past cuts us off from God's strength. We can only continue in our denial when we maintain an image of false strength and self-sufficiency. Denying our anger results in a *counterfeit* forgiveness. Many of us "manufacture" forgiveness in an effort to be obedient, while scrambling to maintain our illusion of self-sufficiency. That false forgiveness leads to legalism, moralism, and false pride.

Forgiveness that follows an honest expression of our hurt and anger is the only kind of forgiveness that makes it possible for us to align our hearts with the gospel. When we relinquish our omnipotence, we can finally acknowledge our true feelings. When we acknowledge our feelings, we admit our vulnerability. And when we admit our vulnerability, we find that we stand in need of a loving God.

Even though many currently popular books and secular

psychologists tell us differently, genuine forgiveness is the only route to complete healing. When we harbor unforgiveness we are—in essence—continuing to allow the person we won't or "can't" forgive, to control us. Until we forgive that person, we can't learn to live entirely in the present because we are not yet finished with the pain of our past.

In forgiving our abusers, we take back the power that God intends for all humans to have—the power to choose to live wholly for Christ. Forgiving, however, does not necessarily have to be followed by "forgetting." There are times when forgetting would be an exceedingly irresponsible act.

Forgiving does not mean that we are obligated to put ourselves or others in danger. An unrepentant sexual perpetrator, for instance, is one who should be avoided altogether. We are under no obligation to associate with that person or to allow our children to do so. We have a moral obligation to report instances of sexual molestation to the authorities regardless of whether we have forgiven that person—particularly if that person currently has any contact whatever with other children. Reporting such instances is not an act of unforgiveness. It is simply good sense.

You may want to ask yourself some questions before you welcome your abuser back into your life:

- Have the people who abused me indicated that they are now able to perceive their actions as having been harmful?
- Have they repented?
- Have they evidenced that repentance by confessing and asking for forgiveness from every person they abused?
- Do I believe they are still likely to hurt me?
- Do I respect myself enough now to stand up for myself if they attempt to abuse me again?

If you are comfortable with your answers to all of these questions, you and your abuser may be ready to begin a relationship once again. If not, your forgiveness for the offender has allowed you to move away from hurt and bitterness and has released you from the bondage of unforgiveness. Leave the offender in God's hands and get on with your life.

LEAVING THE ANGER BEHIND

Releasing our emotions serves two purposes. On a *psychological* level, such a release allows us to circumvent our developmental arrests. Our pent up emotions tend to prevent us from processing new experiences that might help us to "grow up." Once we have expressed them, we are free to substitute healthier relational experiences for the unhealthy ones stored in our memory.

On a *spiritual* level, we learn a new way of relating to God when we risk being transparent with him. We learn that we do, indeed, have significance. We give ourselves the chance to experience his grace in a new way. Revealing our true emotions to God—who is fully aware of them anyway—also removes one more opportunity for Satan to whisper accusations in our ear.

Once we have expressed all the secrets of our hearts to our loving Daddy-God, we have nothing left to hide. There is nothing left for Satan to threaten to expose. In releasing our repressed emotions, we also experience God's forgiveness. We can finally leave behind forever the guilt we have felt over our hidden anger and the resulting bitterness.

What we needed as children was a *sense of significance*. What we settled for was a *sense of power*. Our determination to see ourselves as omnipotent cut us off from our anger. At first we needed to hide our anger because it reminded us of our powerlessness. But in time, we came to see ourselves as frighteningly powerful. What happens when an omnipotent being vents his or her anger? Destruction!

We became afraid that our anger might destroy those around us. Even as children, we understood that such power is too easily abused. We had the examples of the powerful adults in our lives as proof. So we "stuffed" our anger. In our own minds, we had become too powerful to allow ourselves the luxury of anger. As adults we see the folly of that kind of thinking. But as children we believed such magic was possible.

God gave us our emotions to act as a kind of gauge, to let us know how we are doing and warn us when something is wrong. We need to learn to regard our emotions as a call to action. Emotions provide the energy to change our circumstances. Sadness is meant to move us toward comfort. Anger is meant to compel us to defend ourselves against the cause of our pain. Fear is meant to motivate us to seek safety.

Because we live in a fallen world, our emotions certainly are not always a flawless gauge. Children often get angry when they are disciplined, even by loving parents. In that case, the pain they are motivated to defend against is necessary if they are ever going to grow up to be decent, law abiding citizens. Children sometimes fear going to the doctor, despite the fact that the doctor's visit may be necessary to their health.

Because we are sinners, our emotional responses are not always going to motivate us to take appropriate actions. But denying our emotions altogether—just because they sometimes motivate us inappropriately—is like throwing the baby out with the bath water. Knowing that our emotions were given us by God to benefit us rather than to be our undoing, we must learn to listen to what our hearts tell us and compare it to what Scripture tells us.

HOW DO I KNOW WHETHER I AM ANGRY?

Hidden or repressed anger can be identified by analyzing our ways of relating to those around us. Here is a checklist of symptoms to help you identify whether you have hidden anger.

Emotional signs:
Outbursts of rage or excessive irritability over trifles.
Constant anxiety.

Excessive jealousy or suspiciousness.
Moodiness or restlessness.
Being overly sensitive or easily hurt.
Chronic depression (extended periods of feeling "down" for no apparent reason).

Behavioral signs:
Procrastination in imposed tasks.
Perpetual or habitual lateness.
Constant sarcasm, cynicism, or flippancy in conversation.
Indecisiveness.
Being hypercritical or blaming.
Being confused or preoccupied a great deal of the time.
Being accident prone.
Waking up tired rather than rested and refreshed.
Frequent disturbing or frightening dreams.
Liking sadistic or ironic humor.
Frequent head/stomach/back aches or muscular tension.
Frequent thoughts about death.
Overcontrolled, monotone speaking voice.
Insomnia or sleeping excessively.
Clenching jaws or grinding teeth, especially during sleep.
Being easily fatigued.
Getting drowsy at inappropriate times.
Frequent sighing.
Deliberately injuring oneself (cutting, burning, etc.).
Substance abuse.
Insisting on always being "right."
Distancing from others, silence, coldness, indifference.

Common defenses used to keep anger hidden:
Excessive sociability or being overly polite.
Passive/aggressive behavior (resistance, subtle opposition, being contrary).
Compulsiveness.
Constant cheerfulness or smiling while hurting.

OKAY, SO I'M ANGRY—NOW WHAT?

"'In your anger do not sin': Do not let the sun go down while you are still angry, and do not give the devil a foothold" (Eph 4:26-27). Please notice that this Scripture does not tell us not to *be* angry. Rather it tells us not to sin when we *are* angry. We are also advised to deal with our anger immediately or the devil will use it as a foothold in our lives.

Of course, our problem is that we didn't deal with our anger immediately. We didn't know how, and we had no adults in our lives who were capable of modeling the appropriate way to accomplish such a feat. So it is extremely likely that the devil is using our anger as a foothold in our lives. There is nothing we can do about the past. But we can remove Satan's hold on our lives by dealing with our anger now.

So how do we get mad and still like ourselves in the morning? Perhaps first, we need to redefine anger for ourselves. If we see our anger as one of our God-given emotions, then it may be easier for us to see it as a positive force in our lives. Our anger can cause us to make necessary changes in our circumstances in order to remove us from harm. It can help us to assert ourselves in a loving way and to invite others to treat us with respect. Anger can provide us with the impetus to stop thinking like a victim, to stop being a "doormat." In short, it can motivate us to establish necessary and healthy boundaries.

With God's help, we can learn how to make anger a positive force in our lives. But as survivors, most of us have denied our anger for so long—rather than dealing with it before the sun went down—that we have far more pent up anger than we can possibly use in our efforts to establish boundaries. We need to find ways to express our excess anger so that we can successfully remove Satan's foothold in our lives.

There are probably almost as many ways to discharge anger as there are people who need to. Ask your therapist to help you find safe, positive ways in which to express your anger. Here is a list of ideas to get you started:

- Pray. Tell God how you feel. Refuse to feel ashamed.
- Cry.
- Scream (when you're alone or into a pillow if necessary).
- Talk to or yell at an empty chair.
- Run or exercise while talking aloud about your feelings.
- Tear papers.
- Vigorously chew something.
- Kick your mattress while lying on it.
- Write a letter or journal entry.

Whatever you do, try to express your anger as sincere emotion, without analysis. You can take time later to analyze the "what and why" behind your anger. Your heart has been "put on hold" for long enough. Your head will simply have to wait its turn. Keep in mind, however, that the feeling of power you may get from venting your anger can be addicting—especially if you spent your early years feeling powerless. Remaining "stuck" in your anger may "feel good," but is not acceptable behavior for a believer in Christ.

The purpose of finding specific ways in which to express your anger is simply to help rid yourself of the anger you may have denied and "stuffed" down inside when you were a child. You will discover that anger is always a secondary emotion, a response that follows some other very intense emotion, like fear or pain. The sooner you discover the emotion behind the anger and deal with that, the sooner you will be free to get on with your life in Christ.

WHEN WE'RE MAD AT GOD

Many of us may need to admit that we are angry with God before we can get on with our recovery. Most survivors are. In fact, we are usually angry with God, ourselves, and everyone else. If we are to be completely healed, it is essential that we be honest about the anger we feel—including the anger we feel with God. We may have difficulty admitting—even to ourselves—that we are angry with God. Such a thing seems so unthinkable to many of us.

We may be mad at God without even realizing it. There are three common indications that someone is mad at God.

1. Being grudgingly obedient.
2. Wanting to serve God but remaining mistrustful of his promises.
3. Believing what God says, yet remaining disobedient to his commands.

Being begrudging or disobedient is perhaps easier to see as anger than is mistrust. However, the author of Hebrews says, "Anyone who comes to him must [already] believe that he exists and that he rewards those who earnestly seek him" (Heb 11:6). Withholding trust is one way of telling God we don't want to give in to him.

I have seen people's lives transformed when they have admitted to God and to themselves that they were angry with him—and haven't been struck by lightning or plague as a result. The world continues to spin and they continue to see God manifest his love in their lives. That experience alone has the potential to convince us of God's absolute acceptance of us. God will lovingly show us how his truth can be applied to our deficiencies, our character flaws, our anger, our lack of trust.

Whatever anger we feel—whether with God, ourselves, or those around us—can only heal completely when we face that anger, acknowledge it, and work it through to forgiveness. As children we experienced events that set the grief process into motion. Anger is only one step in a grieving process that we have postponed for years. Since we did not feel free to express our anger, we became stalled on that step of the process.

Once our anger has been fully expressed, we need to allow ourselves the "luxury" of completing the grieving process by mourning our losses. In truth, neither our anger nor our mourning is a luxury, but rather a life-and-death matter. Once we have mourned our loss, we are finally free to accept what has happened to us and begin living a truly abundant life in Christ.

A Practical Exercise
✦ ✦ ✦

1. Make a list of the people against whom you harbor anger.

2. Ask God to bring to mind any other names that should be on the list, and add those names.

3. Even after you have forgiven someone in the spiritual realm, you may still need to process your anger on an emotional level. Once you have forgiven those who have wronged you, you are free to process your remaining emotional anger with your therapist. The forgiving is in the present. The emotions are from long ago. Processing your remaining feelings of anger does not negate your forgiveness in the present, but simply allows you to completely release your past. Thus, use one of the examples given as to how to express that anger and then write down your feelings in a journal. Afterwards, pray the following prayer:

> *In the name of the Lord Jesus Christ, I command the spirit of anger to depart from me forever. I order you to go wherever Christ commands you to go. I acknowledge that God alone is all powerful. In the name of Jesus, I renounce any false claim to power that I may have made as a child. I confess any sins I have committed out of anger [list the ones you remember]. I ask forgiveness for those acts. As God has forgiven me, I forgive [list the names of people and what they did]. Amen.*

TWELVE

Ritualized Abuse

Where can I go from your Spirit? Where can I flee from your presence? If I go up to the heavens, you are there; if I make my bed in the depths, you are there. If I rise on the wings of the dawn, if I settle on the far side of the sea, even there your hand will guide me, your right hand will hold me fast. **Psalm 139:7-10**

EVEN AS A TWENTY-FOUR-YEAR-OLD, Phyllis was afraid of everything. Her fear was well hidden, however, both from herself and the world. But I could see many indications of fearfulness during my initial interview with her. Phyllis became agitated over any situation in which she didn't feel that she was in complete control. Anything unfamiliar or unexpected sent her into a panic.

Phyllis remained unconscious of her fearfulness because she kept it hidden through compensating behaviors—hypervigilance and a demanding, critical nature. She required that everything be "just right" at all times. When asked to name her specific fears, Phyllis was conscious of only a few. At the head of the list was an unreasonable fear of animals—particularly dogs. She said she had been afraid of dogs for as long as she could remember.

Her chief complaint when she came to see me was that her short-term memory was becoming shockingly poor. Her more recent memory lapses were clinically intriguing and suggested that she was under extreme stress. Phyllis told me that she had always taken pride in her ability to stay on top of her busy schedule. She spent each evening poring over her appointment book so that she would be aware of everything she had to do, and at what time, the following day. Phyllis felt that her job as a corporate executive simply would not permit her to have any surprises in her day.

Her compulsive behavior wasn't working for her as well as it once had, however. In recent weeks Phyllis had found herself in meetings having no idea why she was there or what the topic was. She was embarrassed to admit that she had arrived at her office one morning, unable to remember what she had done since she awakened that morning—not even certain whether she had showered.

Trips to the market were becoming equally disconcerting. Phyllis said she would often wander the aisles, lost and unable to find what she wanted, despite the fact that she had been shopping in the same store for years. Much to her chagrin, she could name any number of other unexplainable lapses in time and memory.

All of these events, plus other experiences, pointed to a blossoming dissociative thought disorder. Phyllis reported feeling that she was someone else who sat outside, watching her at times. At other times she had the sensation that the world around her wasn't real—that *she* wasn't real.

She sometimes felt as if someone else was living inside her body. She intuitively sensed that other person's presence and felt that the "other" was stronger and braver than she. And when things got to be too stressful for her, it seemed almost as if she stepped back and allowed this "other person" to perform for her. She impressed people with her bravado at those times.

Phyllis' memories of her childhood were very sad. Her parents had been alcoholics who fought constantly. She remembered being the neighborhood stray who spent as much time as she could wandering the neighborhood looking for people to befriend. She had warmed to anyone who would pay attention to her. This little girl remembered being afraid of one neighbor, however. She recalled avoiding his house whenever she was out looking for something to do. This neighbor had several dogs and Phyllis distinctly remembered being terribly afraid of them. But she couldn't remember why. In fact, she recalled her childhood only vaguely. But "all in all," she felt that her "childhood had been okay."

The fact that her experiences of dissociating had become more extreme in the past few months was very interesting. I suspected Post Traumatic Stress Disorder (PTSD). I explained to Phyllis that PTSD is sometimes triggered when repressed memories begin to work their way into the conscious mind. As bits and pieces begin to surface, the survivor experiences heightened fearfulness or agitation.

Present sights or experiences may also be reminders of a past traumatic event, which may cause a previous split in one's personality to manifest itself once again. Phyllis seemed to be suffering from post traumatic blackouts, called fugue states, at increasingly shorter intervals.

I asked Phyllis if any experiences stood out in her mind as possible triggers for her. The only thing she could think of had taken place almost two years prior to her seeing me. Her boyfriend had asked her to dog-sit for him while he was away for three weeks. With growing agitation and animosity, she described being "cooped up" each evening with her boyfriend's German shepherd. She had become depressed and angry, swearing at herself much of the time. She recounted feeling a loathing for the dog and herself whenever the dog tried to get her to pet him.

Phyllis couldn't explain her feelings so she had chosen not to mention her difficulties when her boyfriend returned. A long season of seemingly unrelated psychic disruption followed—culminating, nearly two years later, in distressing lapses of memory.

I asked Phyllis to draw a time line of her life, using butcher paper so that it could be as long as she wished it to be. I told her to mark every significant event—good or bad. Each therapy session, I asked her to lie on my office couch and picture herself roaming her neighborhood as a little girl. The images she remembered were all benign. But I asked her to describe her feelings about each one. In this way we gained access to her emotions in instances that were nonthreatening. This fortified her ability to stay with her emotions—even "unpleasant" ones—without dissociating.

Then one day, she abruptly halted her narrative. She suddenly remembered the "scary" neighbor's house. He had always sat out front on the porch. It was extremely hard for her to "stay with" this image. Phyllis sat up on my couch as she fought the urge to dissociate. She guessed that she must have been about seven or eight years old at the time. She vaguely recalled the color of the house and the fact that the man's beard had been snow-white.

Phyllis brought her completed time line to one of her subsequent sessions. It showed a sharp dip—representing a difficult time—when she was seven years old. She recalled feeling dirty "on the inside," not wanting others to see her shame. She had always assumed she was ashamed of her parents because of their alcoholism.

Phyllis remembered that school had suddenly become very difficult for her during that time. She had isolated herself more and more from her peers at school and had become increasingly infatuated with fantasy, drifting in and out of reality. Her teacher complained of her lack of attentiveness. But the notes her teacher sent home with her were disregarded. She said her parents "were too drunk to care."

As Phyllis continued to talk about her images of the man on the porch, her sense of fear escalated. But her courage to continue was greater. In her next session, I asked Phyllis to picture herself standing on the sidewalk while the old man sat on his porch. I had her engage in a conversation with Jesus Christ, first asking him for courage, and then telling him what frightened her so much about the old man.

In another session, I asked her to imagine herself beginning to move toward the man with Jesus beside her. I told her
to stop each time it became too frightening and ask Jesus for
his strength. Finally the little girl in her imagination reached
the porch and stood next to the old man.

It was then that Phyllis recalled that the old man actually
had invited her up onto the porch. She couldn't remember
what had happened once she had joined him, but she had
the disquieting suspicion that she had gone into the house.
She mentioned, again, how frightening the man's dogs were.
I had her draw pictures of each of them. One of the dogs was
big and black. Phyllis began speaking of that dog as the
man's "devil dog." She said its eyes were cold and dark. Every
time I asked her to picture the dog she said she began to feel
"spacey" inside.

Eventually, Phyllis remembered having been lured into the
man's house with the offer of some fresh baked cookies. He
praised and flattered the emotionally starved little girl. He
plied her with goodies and promised more each time she
returned. The old man gradually broke down her natural
defenses and inspired her trust. Phyllis said that she had
never before felt so "wanted." Then he asked her to pose for
him so that he could have pictures of "such a pretty little
girl." He said he worked for some Hollywood producers.
Another time he asked her to remove just a "little bit" of her
clothing for the pictures because that would be "more excit-
ing." One thing led mercilessly to another. As it turned out,
the man had applied a kind of ritual to his abuse of the little
girl. That ritual involved the use of photographic equipment
to hide his real intent. The ritual suggested that something
important was happening.

It took weeks for the two of us to reach this point in Phyllis'
therapy. Now the therapeutic groundwork we had laid earlier
began to carry us along. Her memory began to come together rapidly. She remembered the old man cajoling her to
stretch out on a mattress—completely nude—so that he

could take pictures. In subsequent photography sessions, he posed her seductively. During one session he invited his black dog into his studio. He promised her money if she would pose provocatively with the dog. As Phyllis told me that, she began to cry. She was finally free to weep the tears of horror and shame that had remained unexpressed for so many years.

Phyllis sobbed loudly as she recounted the way the man had arranged the scene he wanted to photograph. She cried out in anger that the man kept laughing and calling the dog "you little devil" while struggling to gain its cooperation. It seemed that the dog had better sense than the man himself. The dog had found the situation unacceptable and had tried to escape.

Weeks later, after assimilating these memories, Phyllis was able to see why she had secretly believed all those years that the devil (via the black dog) had gotten hold of her and that she was inherently bad. She had relegated this belief to her unconscious, which gave it even more power. This lie had kept her away from church and distant from God. She had always felt that she was ineligible to receive God's love.

Phyllis was also part of a support group I was leading. The members of the group and I encouraged Phyllis to put on the full armor of God. Then we helped Phyllis to voice her anger over what the old man did to her. She successfully took a stand against Satan's lies, just as Ephesians tells us to: "Put on the full armor of God so that you can take your stand against the devil's schemes" (Eph 6:11). Once Phyllis was able to acknowledge her anger and place the blame and shame back on the old man—and on Satan—where it belonged, she was able to begin to take a stand for truth.

It was essential that she stand up for the little girl who had taken on the guilt and shame that actually belonged to an old man. It was equally important for Phyllis to declare the truth of her heart by venting her repressed emotions. Most important, however, was her renunciation, in Jesus' name, of the power and dominion of the lies she had believed.

In the group sessions that followed, the members were

able to help Phyllis see that she had not been to blame—
even though she had not objected to events at the time. She
did not deserve the shame, despite the fact that her body
might have responded to being sexually stimulated.

Phyllis came to see that she was not irrevocably sick, deviant, or reprehensible. She had been a helpless child, victimized by a man who demonstrated by his actions that he was
working with the forces of darkness. Eventually she was able
to weep openly in front of the group and was comforted by
various group members. The incident was no longer a secret.
And neither were her pain and grief.

The healing needed by victims of ritual abuse such as
Phyllis involves correcting a sickness in their souls. This illness is based on the lie that some things are unforgivable.
When children are made to do horrifying things against
God's will and their own higher moral reasoning, then it will
forever- more seem that they have committed the unpardon-
able sin. Their secrets not only shame them, but eternally
condemn them.

God's Word tells us all things are made visible when
brought into the light (see Eph 5:13). This is good medicine
for survivors. When victims tell their secrets, they experience
the reality of God's forgiveness for the first time in their lives.
Satan's hold is loosened when we discover that "he who
knows us best loves us most."

IT'S ALL ABOUT POWER

In the simplest terms, ritualized abuse is any form of abuse
that takes on mechanistic, repetitive, ritualistic, or ceremonial overtones. Ritualized abuse can fall into one of three cat-
egories, but frequently consists of two or all three types.

1. *Religious ritual:* an activity or ceremony with spiritual or
   religious significance such as occult practices and Satan
   worship.

2. *Social ritual:* behavior having a social or moral significance, such as sexual activities involving picture taking or videotaping for child pornography.
3. *Psychological ritual:* repetitive or ritualized acts having emotional significance like "dressing up" for Daddy in Mommy's lingerie.

Ritual abuse of any kind is about power. Perpetrators of this sort of abuse incorporate their pathology into a ceremonial experience in order to claim power. It is an attempt to gain power over one's own impulses, over the victim, or both. In *Cults That Kill,* a young person talks about Satanism:

> What I like about Satanism is the power that it gives me. The people at school know I'm into it and they don't mess with me…. It also gives me the feeling that I can do anything I put my mind to…. The other religions don't teach you that. They teach you to be humble and love one another. Why should I love anyone else? All people want is to get as much as they can. That's the way life is. Satanism has taught me about life. It helps you grow up.[1]

The same book notes the observations of a police detective: "People aren't satisfied to live within an environment they have created. It's not enough to have power over themselves. They want to control the heavens and each other. As the need for more power grows, occult crime increases. It attracts people who want more power."[2]

As victims of ritualized abuse are overpowered, their wills are stripped away in numerous important areas of their lives. While survivors of all types of abuse can rightfully say that their wills have been violated, survivors of ritualized abuse often have their wills reshaped or programmed in specific ways. Mind-altering, mood-altering, and life-changing techniques are used to force the victim into submission—obtaining the victim's cooperation in what would otherwise be repugnant acts or beliefs.

These brainwashing techniques can include drugs, the power of suggestion, behavior modification, pleasure/pain association, sleep or food deprivation, and so forth. Programming always involves the use of fear or false hope as a motivating force. The victim's thinking and emotions are effected in such a way that his or her contact with time, space, and self is challenged.

This process results in confusion regarding the difference between right and wrong and a sense of unreality during the traumatic events. The fragmentation of the victim's personality—ranging from dissociative states to Multiple Personality Disorder—is common especially when painful stimuli are introduced. Ritualized abuse of a pseudo-religious nature also leaves survivors to deal with continued demonic activity in their lives. Any false religion carries Satan's stamp of approval and continued interest.

Satanic rituals and cults dehumanize their victims in their acts of worship. In fact, satanists see their victims as simply a means to an end—bereft of humanity. Their victim's emotional and physical pain is regarded as inconsequential in light of their "greater" goal. It may seem incomprehensible that any human being could completely disregard the pain of another. But when we understand the mind-set of the satanist, it doesn't seem so farfetched.

The U.S. government "Handbook for Chaplains," prepared by the Church of Satan in an effort to present their church as a recognized, respectable alternative religion, summarizes the ethical stance of the Church of Satan with "Nine Satanic Statements."

The Nine Satanic Statements

1. Satan represents indulgence instead of abstinence!
2. Satan represents vital existence, instead of spiritual pipe dreams!
3. Satan represents undefiled wisdom, instead of hypocritical self-deceit!

4. Satan represents kindness to those who deserve it, instead of love wasted on ingrates!
5. Satan represents vengeance instead of turning the other cheek!
6. Satan represents responsibility to the responsible, instead of concern for psychic vampires!
7. Satan represents man as just another animal, sometimes better, sometimes worse than those that walk on all fours, who, because of his "divine spiritual and intellectual development," has become the most vicious animal of all!
8. Satan represents all of the so-called sins, as they all lead to physical, mental and emotional gratification!
9. Satan has been the best friend the church has ever had, as he has kept it in business all these years![3]

Because satanists call upon the forces of darkness for their power, demonic activity is an inherent part of their rituals and lifestyles. In fact, Multiple Personality Disorders may sometimes develop as a result of demonic activity on a psychological level. Timothy Maas, Ph.D., is quoted as saying, "The cultists have known about multiple personalities for hundreds of years.... They have formalized it [through programming techniques] now to where they can literally create multiple personalities."[4]

Those who are ritually abused are made to feel cut off from the outside world, either momentarily or permanently. As a result, they may begin to look to the cult or their abusers for support or, at the very least, survival. Victims often feel that the perpetrator has the power of life and death over them—in fact, that may be true—and so victims become grateful for any favor shown. They may even begin to identify with or join the "cause" of the perpetrator.

Even when the concessions made by the victim are completely unconscious, certain behaviors or attitudes may become manifest as a result. Behaviors may include being drawn to things of darkness such as crystals, tarot cards, group sex, sadomasochism, ouija boards, palm reading, and the like. Attitudinal concessions may include hating authority, opposing social mores, disdaining things of a religious nature, and so forth.

Rituals tend to codify what one has experienced. The victim—especially one who is a child—comes to believe that the experience or statements made are inviolate and forever true. This makes it even more difficult to get past the defenses and change behaviors and attitudes resulting from ritualized abuse—or even to identify the lies the survivor still believes on an unconscious level.

Survivors of satanic ritualistic abuse exhibit symptoms which are often a symbolic reenactment of their abuse. They suffer from fear of groups, fear of blood, fear of animals, fear of being lost, claustrophobia, etc. A fear of rituals themselves may cause a survivor of such abuse to avoid church attendance. Even Christian church services involve certain rituals, such as taking communion. Survivors of this type of abuse are easily triggered. They often demonstrate a strong tendency toward numbing strategies or dissociation as a defense.

Satanic ritual abuse victims are frequently taught that secrecy is absolutely necessary to their survival or to the survival of those they love. So it becomes even more difficult for them to break their silence than with other forms of abuse. And, since they have become so convinced that acknowledging the truth is life-threatening, they may dissociate whenever they are triggered, rather than take the chance of remembering what has happened to them.

Even when a satanic ritual abuse survivor does finally remember the ritualized abuse, he or she may feel forced to "take flight" through dissociation or other forms of distancing strategies when pressed to talk about past events. Those who have been ritually abused by satanic groups isolate and insulate themselves from others and from reality.

A child who is being ritually abused in some sort of cult is frequently told that the group will "know" if the child tells the secret. Consequently, such a child may fear that an accidental "slip" could result in his death. "Splitting" is one way for such children to remain "safe." He can't tell what he doesn't know. Splitting can be accomplished through dissociation or through fragmentation of the personality. Splitting also offers children a means of "escaping" the horrors of the abuse they are forced to endure. When they have endured all they are able to, they can split off and allow another part of themselves to "take over."

"Multiple Personality Disorder" (MPD) is sometimes a byproduct of splitting. However, not everyone who dissociates has this disorder. MPD is generally regarded as an unconscious response to trauma that results in the fragmentation of one's personality. That fragmentation causes secondary personalities to develop. If a survivor of satanic ritual abuse has developed a split personality, those personalities or fragments may surface much later in life through post traumatic shock.

BREAKING THE CODE

Survivors of satanic ritual abuse have an even more complicated "code" of symptoms than survivors of other sorts of abuse. It is not uncommon for a child who is being abused by a cult to be given an "object lesson" about what happens to people who "tell." They may be forced to watch as another child is murdered because this other child "told the secret." As a result they generally invest more of their energy in camouflaging their secret than do survivors of other forms of abuse.

Of crucial importance is that satanic ritual abuse survivors often continue to be targets for ongoing spiritual assault. They often feel soiled, evil, and untouchable—completely separated from God. Such victims need to establish a sense of reality in Christ by methodically replacing their false perceptions with the truth about who they are as a son or daughter of God. Identifying those lies, however, takes prayer and patience. They are frequently so deeply buried in the survivor's unconscious mind that the survivor seems to possess a sort of "double" reality.

On a conscious level, one middle-aged woman knew and believed that her body was the temple of the Holy Spirit. Then one day she happened to "stumble" across a memory of having "prayed" to Satan. Having been young enough to need assistance in saying the prayer, she had been led through it in a repeat-after-me fashion. This woman remembered asking Satan to come and dwell within her, making her the embodiment of evil.

Suddenly, she realized why she continued to feel that she needed to kill her body in order to be "completely free of evil." On an unconscious level, this Christian woman had continued to believe that the prayer she had said as a small child still held some power over her. Once it was exposed to the light of God's Word, she was able to refute it and never again fell prey to the feeling that she needed to die.

Survivors of satanic ritual abuse need their feelings of grief, anger, and betrayal affirmed. In this way they can separate themselves—in their own minds—from their abusers. Until those emotions are validated and fully acknowledged, such survivors often feel they are still "one of them" even when they have no continuing contact with cult members. When they are able to acknowledge their true feelings of horror, dread, and fear over what their abusers did, they can fully appreciate that they were victims rather than willing participants.

When an SRA survivor experiences a spiritual assault, observers may come to the conclusion that his or her psychotic-like, self-destructive behaviors are evidence of a strictly emotional disorder. While such behaviors can be due to the emotional damage the survivor has sustained, that isn't necessarily the case. A spiritual cause should be seriously considered.

These survivors may experience a continued sense of foreboding and fearfulness. Their fantasies and dreams may be horrifying and dark. Their image of God is often highly distorted. They may voice a hatred or fear of Christ—regarding him as unsafe, a sexual deviant, and so forth.

One young woman had been brainwashed as a child into believing that the man who came to molest her during rituals was "Christ" and the man who comforted her afterward was "Lucifer." The molestation was called being "saved." So when the man labeled as "Christ" came to "save" this little girl, he was actually sexually torturing her. Other such diabolical programming is commonly reported by survivors of this kind of abuse.

Repressed memories may suddenly surface years after the original trauma. For example, an article in the *L.A. Times* reported "a forty-eight-year-old woman testified that she had been forced to murder her own baby during a satanic ritual in a secret cave more than thirty-five years ago." The woman stated that "she had repressed the memories of her childhood and only began to remember them in mid-1988, six months after she began psychotherapy for marital counseling."[5]

The SRA survivor needs to have the opportunity to reassimilate his or her past through the recovery of memories. At the same time, it would be misleading to believe that recurring, horrifying images that seem to plague a survivor are nothing more than a simple release of a memory. They can be a form of spiritual harassment. If such images are tormenting the survivor rather than providing release or enlightenment, they should be suspect.

Survivors of satanic ritual abuse especially need to learn to "fight the good fight" by being fully equipped with the armor of God. They should be taught how to spot the falsehoods they have believed. And they need to be taught how to resist them by declaring the truth from God's Word. They also need to be encouraged to renounce false beliefs about love, safety, God, their own guilt, and so on.

Most important, God's truth needs to be spoken out loud so that every lying spirit can hear. While evil spirits can't read our thoughts they must obey our commands in the name of Jesus Christ. It is essential for survivors of satanic ritual abuse to break their silence and give up the secrets. Their previously repressed grief, anger, and need for comfort must replace their numbing shame.

FROM DARKNESS TO LIGHT

Victims of ritualized abuse of any kind must rediscover their emotions by reconnecting with their previously silent hearts. They need to weave together the lost parts of their past to form a cohesive picture as they recover bits of memory. They must be reprogrammed, which is not a simple task. To that end, the tools of their faith need to be reclaimed.

When abused in a pseudo-religious context, survivors may need to reprogram themselves in regard to any number of symbols used within the Christian church—from crosses to anointing oil—all of which are routinely defiled by satanists. They need to deliberately learn to associate the concept of the shed blood with Christ's redemption rather than the horrifying, gory sacrifices they may have witnessed. They need to sensitize themselves to the true meaning of the elements of communion, while desensitizing themselves to the horrible pictures that assault their minds as a result of the mock-communion services in which they may have been forced to participate.

Survivors of ritual abuse may be harassed by spirits of darkness who must be confronted, and the lies those spirits use as strongholds must be brought into the light of the Word of God. These victims often have a number of misperceptions about Satan and his demons. They frequently see Satan as God's equal—omniscient and omnipresent. They perceive themselves to be surrounded by demons and powerless to drive them away. As a result their biggest challenge is overcoming fear. They must learn to deal with fear fearlessly.

It is important for a survivor of satanic ritual abuse to come to an understanding of Satan's limitations. He or she must become convinced that Satan and his army of demons are finite beings, limited by time and space. They can't be all places at once. They can't read minds. They can't force us to do something against our will. Evil spirits must deal in trickery and deceit rather than force.

Once we learn their tricks and recognize and refute their lies, Satan and his demons are rendered powerless in our lives. To that end, a helpful approach is for the survivor to specifically renounce any vows taken. And demonic assignments against them and their family line must be broken through prayer.

SHARING OUR COMFORT

Dr. Julias Segal, in a book entitled *Winning Life's Toughest Battles*, lists five elements needed in order to recover from a traumatic event. They apply to all survivors of abuse, but particularly to survivors of ritual abuse. His list includes: communication; control; conviction; a clear conscience; and compassion.[6]

Dr. Segal's first element is *communication*. By choosing to interact with others rather than withdraw, we demonstrate a willingness to do something about our suffering. We invite support and others' insights regarding our suffering.

Second is the sense that God has everything in *control*. Survivors almost always see their world as out of control and highly unpredictable, which adds to our sense of fear and internalized stress. While we may not have the perspective to see God's purpose in allowing events to take place, we can be sure that he has our best interests at heart.

Dr. Segal addresses *conviction* by quoting Carl Jung: "Meaning makes a great many things endurable—perhaps everything." Christians are in a unique position to hold the conviction that our suffering has purpose. God has promised to do all things for our good, in order to help us become a better reflection of his Son, Jesus Christ. That knowledge has the power to help us see that we did more than simply survive. Although survival—particularly in the case of those who have endured ritual abuse—is a great feat in itself, there is *purpose* in our survival. We are *more than conquerors* (see Rom 8:37).

If we are to be more than survivors, we need to have a *clear conscience*. The secrets we carry are invariably infused with shame. Our secrets provide a foothold for Satan. Confession is the key. When a survivor confesses the act he or she may have been forced to do during rituals, or that happened in the course of other forms of abuse, then that foothold is removed. Satan can no longer plague these victims by whispering condemning statements to them. Confession sheds light on the darkness in our minds and hearts and releases us from spiritual captivity.

Finally, *compassion* is a tremendously important ingredient in our recovery. Immense healing becomes available to us when we demonstrate God's love through our compassion. The Apostle Paul puts it this way: "Praise be to the God and Father of our Lord Jesus Christ, the Father of compassion and the God of all comfort, who comforts us in all our troubles, so that we can comfort those in any trouble with the comfort we ourselves have received from God" (2 Cor 1:3-4).

When we share the comfort we have received from God, we are affirming our recovery, acknowledging our gratefulness to God for what he has accomplished in our lives, and facilitating our further recovery... all in one simple action of compassion.

WHEN MEMORIES AREN'T MEMORIES

We need to keep in mind that the recovery of repressed memories does not constitute recovery from abuse. Even though memories can be important, they are not essential. God's truth is what brings about our recovery by setting us free from bondage to the powers of darkness.

Memories are not always clear or reliable. As I mentioned in the chapter on the inner child, what we remember is bound to be colored by the perceptions of the child we were when the event occurred. One young woman who was ritually abused recalled seeing "trees on fire" during one of the rituals. As an adult, she came to the conclusion that what she had really seen were people with flashlights sitting in the trees overhead. Our memories of an event are limited by the cognitive skills we possessed at the time of the event.

Just because some memories are born of fantasy, the survivor should not be considered a liar. "Fantasy memories" may be the way survivors defend themselves against the genuine pain that the truth would surely bring to the surface. In such an instance, survivors can vent a small portion of that pain while protecting themselves from the full burden of their true pain. Lurking underneath that fantasy memory may be milestone shame which is yet to be uncovered.

Charlotte came to me already convinced that she was a victim of satanic ritual abuse. She had numerous memories of the rituals she had endured. But the recovery of these memories had afforded her no symptomatic relief. In fact, Charlotte was obsessing about them. It seemed that she was being buried under a deeper and deeper pile of unresolved feelings and issues. With the recovery of each "new" memory, her condition grew worse rather than better. And her thought processes were becoming more muddled rather than clearer.

I questioned Charlotte about when these memories had begun to surface and what she might have been discussing with her previous therapist at the time. She said they had discussed some remote, foggy memories of her grandfather, who lived with her family, visiting her room to say goodnight. His hand would draw pictures on her back until she fell asleep. She and her counselor never examined those memories any further, however, because horrifying images of cult activities began to surface shortly afterward.

I needed to be very sensitive to Charlotte and proceed slowly. She was trying desperately to access and vent the strong feelings of horror and grief that had resulted from her molestation, without betraying her beloved "Granddaddy." Eventually, Charlotte was able to admit what had actually happened. Then she was able to completely release her shame and grief because she had finally tapped into them by acknowledging the real abuse she had suffered. In Charlotte's case, her memories of ritualized abuse had only been a decoy that needed to be interpreted in the context of a loyal little girl trying to heal while continuing to carry her secret.

Researchers have discovered recently that post-traumatic memories can change when additional information about an event is added to what the survivor already knows. When additional information is integrated with existing memories, the mind uses it to supplement and alter what a person recollects.

Given this new research, it is important to measure the validity of recovered memories against what is *known* to be true about a person's life, looking for both historical and experiential corroboration. We can safely assume memories to be real when their recovery provides some symptomatic relief and/or greater illumination of other related, unrepressed memories.

When memories are genuine, survivors frequently have an "Ah ha!" reaction upon recovering them. Suddenly other events that were never forgotten but were always puzzling, begin to fit easily into the bigger picture of the survivor's life. Certain fears or inexplicable reactions to particular circumstances are suddenly explainable and lose their power to evoke unwanted reactions and emotions. In those instances, the survivor can be sure that the recovered memory is authentic.

We must be sure, however, to treat "fantasy memories" respectfully. If we are patient and sensitive, chances are we can learn something of importance even from them. Let me hasten to say, however, that I believe many of the people who remember suffering ritualized abuse actually have.

Survivors of ritualized abuse are coming forward with increasing frequency. More than ever, Christians need to learn the essentials of spiritual warfare. Secular psychologists have not had a great deal of success with clients who have been ritually abused. Their lack of success can be directly attributed to a lack of the spiritual dimension in their treatment programs.

The Christian community has the opportunity to fill that void. We can supply the answers that the world is seeking. We can speak the truth in love and allow ourselves to be used so that Christ's words will be made manifest: "But I, when I am lifted up from the earth, will draw all men to myself" (Jn 12:32).

A Practical Exercise
✦ ✦ ✦

You can be confident in claiming God's protection regardless of the sort of abuse or neglect you may have experienced as a child. Here is a prayer that may be helpful as you claim that protection.

Because Jesus is my Lord and savior, my body is the temple of the Holy Spirit. I am a citizen in God's kingdom and his own dear child. I acknowledge God's faithfulness. I claim his promise to strengthen me and protect me from evil (2 Thes 3:3).

I declare in the name of the Lord Jesus Christ that Satan and his demons are finite beings who have no power over me. I claim the glory of the Lord as my rear guard (Is 58:8). Heavenly Father, send your angels to encircle and protect me (Ps 34:7; 91:11). I affirm that you have not given me the spirit of fear but of power and of love and of a sound mind (2 Tm 1:7).

I thank you that the weapons of our warfare are not of the flesh, but are mighty through God to the pulling down of strongholds and the casting down of imaginations and every lofty thing raised up against the knowledge of God (2 Cor 10:4-5). Through the power given me in the name of the Lord Jesus Christ, I crush the strongholds Satan may have erected in my life. I bring the blood of Jesus Christ between me and the forces of evil. Amen

THIRTEEN

We Are the Victors!

The chariots of God are tens of thousands and thousands of thousands; the Lord has come from Sinai into his sanctuary. When you ascended on high, you led captives in your train;...

Psalm 68:17-18

A NNE HAD ENDURED extremely poor health during childhood. Her teachers all knew her to be accident prone as well. She remembered being afraid of absolutely everything as a child. As an adult, Anne had frequent bouts with asthma, pneumonia, and bronchitis. Degenerative arthritis, severe chronic depression and anxiety, back trouble, and Temporal Mandibular Joint pain (TMJ) all plagued her.

Even though Anne's body was always covered with bruises, she had absolutely no idea how she sustained any of them. She said she had such a high threshold of pain, that she could bump herself hard enough to cause a large bruise, or even cut herself, without being consciously aware of it. She might not notice a cut until she was inconvenienced by the blood that was oozing from it.

During the course of her therapy, I discovered that Anne had been molested by most of the members of her extended family. Raped by a neighbor when she was just eleven, the young girl had repressed the trauma so quickly that she didn't remember it by the time she arrived home minutes later. Anne became pregnant as a result of the rape. She was too young to realize she was pregnant and because of her youth her parents assumed that she was just putting on weight. Her mother was shocked when Anne went into labor and gave birth to a baby boy.

Believing it would be easier for Anne to put the incident behind her if she never held her baby, the mother turned a deaf ear to Anne's entreaties to give her the baby. She watched, sobbing, as her mother placed a piece of plastic over the baby's face and suffocated him. Shortly after that, Anne repressed the memory of her pregnancy and the birth of her son. Now, years later, she was grieving the death of a son she had never held in her arms.

Anne's parents had taught her that God makes bad things happen to people because he "loves them and wants to teach them a lesson." She naturally concluded that she needed to avoid catching God's attention so that he wouldn't "lovingly" teach her any more lessons. Any more of that sort of "love" might render her life unbearable.

Consequently, Anne spent much of her time trying to avoid noticing when she did something wrong. If she didn't "notice," then she wouldn't have to confess her sin. Then maybe God wouldn't notice either and decide it was time for another "lesson." Anne also avoided asking God for "too much," fearful he would decide it was time for a "lesson" about greediness.

Although she regarded herself as a Christian, her entire spiritual life had become one of avoidance. Now, as an adult, Anne realized that God had not taken her baby's life in order to teach her a lesson. But he was able to *use* the death of her child in order to teach and mold her—a subtle distinction that most children don't comprehend.

During her months in therapy, Anne struggled with her anger toward God. She now knew that God had not *caused* such a tragedy, but could not escape the fact that he had *allowed* it. Anne grappled with finding a way to joyfully worship a God who had allowed her baby to die, all alone and straining to draw breath. For a while she couldn't get past the notion that Satan had won and—out of either impotence or negligence—God had let him. She felt powerless because she saw God as powerless and constantly fought the overwhelming urge to give up. What was the use?

We needed to find a way to correct this new, and equally inaccurate, perception of God. I asked Anne to envision the birth of her baby and ask Christ, "Where were you when this happened to me?" Immediately, Christ showed her where he had been. In her mind's eye, Anne saw Christ standing by, weeping, as her baby died. She saw him take her baby in his arms so that he could return to heaven with the baby and care for him.

Anne had her answer. The Lord was telling her, "Right there. I was right there with you." God had not ignored her pain. In fact, it was in that instant that Christ's words took on new meaning for her: "I tell you the truth, whatever you did for one of the least of these brothers of mine, you did for me" (Mt 25:40).

It took many months for Anne to complete her grieving process. She had to take a stand against every lie she found operating in her life. During those months she learned to appreciate God's view of things. Humans view things in terms of "day-tight compartments." God sees things in terms of eternity. Anne realized that her loss was only temporary. One day in heaven, she would get to hold her baby.

ONLY BELIEVE

Many of us have learned to embrace the safety to be found in anonymity. As children, we often realized that if we could avoid attracting attention, we could avoid abuse—whether at home or at school. Unfortunately, we carry that sort of reasoning into our relationship with our heavenly Father as well. Somewhere in our unconscious mind, we still believe that if we don't mention to our Daddy that we blew it, he may not notice. If we don't confess to him a wrong attitude, God won't know about it.

We still believe in a God that demands harsh penance, someone who demands sacrifice before he is willing to label us "good." When the crowd at Capernaum asked Jesus Christ, "'What must we do to do the works God requires?' Jesus answered, 'The work of God is this: to believe in the one he has sent'" (Jn 6:28-29). Simply believe.

Certainly, our love for God and our gratitude for having been redeemed and healed through his Son will spur us on to other good works. "For we are God's workmanship, created in Christ Jesus to do good works, which God prepared in advance for us to do" (Eph 2:10). But, as survivors of abuse and neglect, we need to be particularly mindful of God's grace and his acceptance of us—*just as we are.*

Our consciousness of God's grace will enable us to stand without fear under God's benevolent gaze. As we willingly bare our souls before God, asking him to purify and correct us, we will find a new strength and courage with which to face our enemy, the devil. In doing so, we deprive Satan of any moral footing where he can operate.

In order to be able to face the enemy, we must be able to face ourselves. And it is so much easier to face one's worst character flaws when we have a loving Father quietly reiterating, "There is now no condemnation for those who are in Christ Jesus" (Rom 8:1). We can freely confess to God the ways we fall short, because we know that only through his Son, Jesus Christ, can we be changed. As those changes gradually manifest themselves in our lives, "He is faithful and just and will forgive us our sins and purify us from all unrighteousness" (1 Jn 1:9).

KNOWING OUR ENEMY

Satan carried out his plan of destruction for our lives by creating circumstances that caused us to embrace falsehoods, while at the same time assaulting our emotional and social development. We began to perceive everything else that happened to us through a filter formed of those lies. Satan reinforced those misbeliefs by keeping us in the company of spiritual powers that may have become familiar to our families generations before. He further supported them through our scripts and vicious cycles.

More important, Satan kept us believing that we were completely alone—there was no one there for us and there never would be. He kept us striving to provide for our own safety by denying who we were, what we felt, and what we longed for. The drumbeat of fear pounding in our minds drowned out the sound of our own heartbeat. We became convinced that we needed to lie—even to ourselves—in order to survive.

Through this process, denial and repression became woven into the fabric of our lives. And, because all of creation must ultimately be obedient to God, our minds and bodies labored to tell the truth in the only way left—through symbolism—the symbolism of our behavior and our physical ailments.

As we learned to cope with a world which seemed to be beyond our ability to understand, we embraced a web of lies that dictated a need to be either invincible or helplessly incapable—or both, alternately. Either way, we abandoned reality in favor of the falsehoods we thought would provide us some safety, however meager. In the process, we embraced untruths about God's character and his feelings toward us. Self-condemnation, fear, and overwhelming shame became motivating forces in our lives. We developed an overriding need to be needed in order to feel safe.

It is important for us to see that while we may have felt hopeless and abandoned, we were "... hard pressed on every side, but not crushed; perplexed, but not in despair; persecuted, but not abandoned; struck down, but not destroyed" (2 Cor 4:8-9). Our release has already been purchased for us with Christ's blood. We can claim that release when we break through our denial system, identify the scripts and vicious cycles in our lives, and assault the strongholds of darkness with God's truth.

Every lie we have embraced must be spiritually defeated. As God's soldiers, we need to march out against the enemy. We do that through prayer. Every time we discover a falsehood operative in our lives, it is wise to prayerfully examine the possibility that a spirit may have been using it to keep a door "propped open" in our lives. That won't prove to be true in each and every instance. Even so, *any* lie we embrace —even inadvertently—allows the powers of darkness the space to operate at least indirectly in our lives.

RECEIVING OUR MARCHING ORDERS

Our marching orders are clear. The Lord has commanded us to advance against the enemy and "forcefully" take the kingdom. We accomplish this through prayer. In Matthew, we read: "From the days of John the Baptist until now, the kingdom of heaven has been forcefully advancing, and forceful men lay hold of it" (Mt 11:12).

We become forceful by way of truth when we enter into prayer. God wants us to be clear in our minds and convicted in our hearts as to what Satan's lies have done. We also need to be determined in our wills to take hold of the truth as our source of victory.

The Old Testament prophet Daniel offers us an excellent example of how the soldier of God is to enter into prayerful combat with the enemy. Daniel had been taken captive by the Babylonians along with all of Isreal. Led into exile by Nebuchadnezzar, the imprisonment of the Israelites lasted over seventy years. We find Daniel fasting, in sackcloth and ashes, beseeching God to release his chosen people from captivity (see Dn 9).

Daniel's prayer put him squarely in the care of his Father, where, as a son, he could plead with his Father for help and cry out the pain of his heart. He was ready to confess to the

Lord his own deficiencies, as well as those of his fellow Jewish captives. Daniel acknowledged that God had justly scattered the people of Israel because of their unfaithfulness, but also proclaimed that God was merciful and forgiving (see Dn 9:1-19).

Daniel did not attempt to hide from God. He was ready and willing to confess the nation's sin and shame because of their rebellion. This act of trust meant that Daniel was ready to receive God's cleansing. Only then would he be ready to do battle with the enemy, having allowed God to equip him with the truth of the Father's love for his children. More importantly, he had studied God's word and could reiterate God's promises—he knew the truth.

Daniel was also able to discern that it was the "sins and iniquities of our fathers" which made Jerusalem and God's people an object of scorn (Dn 9:16). We also must be able to discern in our spirits the fact that we have been "visited" by our father's sins. Daniel's prayer shows us the importance of seeing how our spiritual ancestry and likeness is born out of visitation by darkness.

Daniel's closing words offer us a model of prayer in marching out to do battle with the enemy.

> Now, our God, hear the prayers and petitions of your servant. For your sake, O Lord, look with favor on your desolate sanctuary. Give ear, O God, and hear; open your eyes and see the desolation of the city that bears your Name. We do not make requests of you because we are righteous, but because of your great mercy. O Lord, listen! O Lord, forgive! O Lord, hear and act! For your sake, O my God, do not delay, because your city and your people bear your Name. **Dn 9:17-19**

If we are to take ground back from the enemy, we must see God as our only resource. Our heavenly Father is our "point man" who goes before us into battle. Prayer fosters this crucial dependency on God. In chapter nine, Daniel's forceful plea demonstrates several important elements:

1. A willingness to confess disobedience (vs. 5).
2. A readiness to receive God's forgiveness for that disobedience (vs. 9).
3. A willingness to acknowledge powerlessness (vs. 11-12).
4. A reliance on God's strength—like Daniel we must acknowledge that it is God's mercy and grace which will gain us the victory over the enemy (vs. 16).
5. Discerning the bondage of ancestral past and declaring that God is ready to do something about it (vs. 16).
6. Identifying God's character, and more importantly, stating truth about what it means to be God's child (vs. 18).

This last point may be the most important. Daniel was claiming his birthright in the Lord as a child of God. As would any child who is loved by his father, Daniel was ready to ask for God's attention. Our heavenly Father is not *compelled* to act on our behalf because of what we have done or ever will do for him.

Therein lies the good news. We no longer need to look at our past as something condemning, something which God holds against us. Our future rests in his arms as we nestle close to God's heart and admit that we need him. We do not need to be strong, capable, self-sufficient, or independent. We simply need to be ready to admit our need and seek God's readiness to respond.

As Christians, we are truly God's children bearing his name. God *wants* to love us. He doesn't need to be *talked into it*. Prayer brings us into God's throne room of grace and makes his help immediately available (see Heb 4:16).

While the battle is the Lord's, we must be discerning in order to test all spirits and carry out our general's command to advance. We have come to understand how our spiritual ancestry brings along with it a lineage of lies. The influence of familiar spirits must be seen and understood and openly challenged.

Through *prayer and fasting*, I believe that the sins of our fathers can be recognized and their influence over us finally ended. We will be able to see familiar spirits operating in our lives in some very specific ways. They will come by way of spiritual assignments. They may exist within a spirit of influence over us simply because of inner vows of allegiance we may have made as victims. Whatever contracts have allowed them to remain a part of our lives—things negotiated by way of our subtle agreement with their influence—must be broken in Jesus' name.

> When you were dead in your sins and in the uncircumcision of your sinful nature, God made you alive with Christ. He forgave us all our sins, having canceled the written code, with its regulations, that was against us and that stood opposed to us; he took it away, nailing it to the cross. And having disarmed the powers and authorities, he made a public spectacle of them, triumphing over them by the cross. **Col 2:13-15**

THE LANGUAGE OF LOVE

In essence, we have been taught a foreign language by the father of lies. It is the language we speak to ourselves. Satan's native tongue is a language of self-hatred and despair, a tongue alien to our heavenly Father. We need to study a new language, the language of love.

Just as we would need to be patient with ourselves in learning an earthly language, we also need to be patient with ourselves in learning God's native tongue. No matter what we may have suffered, we can be absolutely sure that God can and will mold our experiences in a way that will enable us to be an example of his character and a witness to his glory. We need simply to learn how to share our hearts with him.

Remember that healing is a process. We need not concern ourselves with how long that process may take, only with keeping our focus on our loving Father. He will—quite literally—take care of all the rest. The spiritual war in which we find ourselves is already won. And our heavenly Father is ready to lead us into the skirmishes that remain before us. We fight our battles within the shadow of the cross. We are guaranteed the victory: "Being confident of this, that he who began a good work in you will carry it on to completion until the day of Christ Jesus" (Phil 1:6). We need no longer be afraid, angry, or sad because God intends to be our glory and the lifter of our heads (see Ps 3:3). Our hearts can be reconciled to the Father, because as his children we can finally *know* the truth of his love for us—a love for which he was willing to die.

A Practical Exercise

✦ ✦ ✦

Claim a blessing from God by praying the following prayer:

Father, I know that I am your beloved child because your Word tells me so. I also know that you have provided me with the power, through the name of your Son, to order the forces of evil to depart from me forever. I do so now, in the power of that name which is above all names, Jesus Christ.

Lord, I give my life to you. I accept all that has occurred in my life as having been a part of your ultimate plan. And I ask that you continue to use the suffering in my life to produce perseverance and character, which lead to hope.

I thank you that you are already redeeming the promise from Joel 2:25 that says: "I will repay you for the years the locusts have eaten." And I thank you for the special strength and the understanding for others that have become a part of my life as a result of the pain of my past. I claim your blessing through your Son, Christ Jesus. Amen.

What to Look for in a Therapist

IF YOU ARE A SURVIVOR OF ABUSE or neglect, you need someone in your corner, preferably someone who has been
trained to deal with recovery issues. But looking for the right
therapist can seem like an overwhelming task. So much
seems to be at stake. This becomes a particularly daunting
task if you happen to be depressed or in the midst of a crisis.

The following suggestions certainly aren't the last word on
choosing a therapist. They should be adapted to your individual needs, but perhaps they can help to make the task a little
easier. Once you have chosen a therapist, remember that you
don't take a vow to remain with that person until "death do
you part." If you later discover that he or she isn't quite right
for you, you are free to look for someone else.

Also, a therapist may be exactly right for you at one stage
of your recovery and not right for another. Try to be flexible,
yet aware of your motivation for wanting to switch. Determine whether your desire to change stems from a greater—
or at least different—awareness of your needs, or whether
you may just be running from the depth of relationship that
may be developing. Getting close is often scary for survivors.
Yet that is exactly what we need.

So be kind to yourself. Don't remain with a therapist who
is simply not right for you. But don't run from a relationship
because trust is developing and you aren't yet comfortable
with trust. Sometimes a "leap of faith" is the appropriate next
step in recovery work.

Don't hesitate to tell a therapist that you want to schedule an initial appointment in order to interview him or her. No true professional will object to such an interview. During that initial appointment, you will want to ask a number of questions to help you ascertain how well you might be able to work with this therapist. Be honest about whatever causes your red flags to go up regarding the therapist and his or her way of relating to you. The way in which the therapist handles that sort of honesty can tell you a great deal about that person.

Therapists should be willing and able to state clearly their fees. Also clear should be the "ground rules" in regard to canceling appointments, calling after hours, what arrangements can be made for dealing with crisis situations, and so forth. During the day, you should be able to reach your therapist by means of office staff or an answering service.

If the therapist has an answering machine rather than an answering service, does the answering machine message include a number you can call in case of emergencies? A therapist who is completely inaccessible outside of office hours is not likely to be one you will feel comfortable with. Those who routinely give their home phone numbers to clients, however, are probably not right for you either. A therapist with good boundaries is one who will be able to model appropriate behavior for you. You are not looking for a stern taskmaster nor an emotionally unavailable person. Neither are you looking for someone who will be your buddy. You can find buddies elsewhere.

You can ask what experience therapists have had with role playing, and whether they have facilitated or participated in groups employing techniques like family sculpting and psychodrama. The more therapeutic techniques they are comfortable using, the more likely they will be able to pinpoint what you need at any given time. You may also want to ask whether that therapist is prepared to provide a safe atmosphere in which to do anger work.

Don't hesitate to ask a few personal questions in order to

ascertain how open the therapist is willing to be with you. It is not appropriate to ask immensely personal questions, of course, but asking whether he or she is married or has any children is perfectly acceptable. In that way you can also determine whether that person will have an experiential understanding of the marriage and parenting issues you may bring up in the course of therapy.

A therapist who is unwilling to be self-disclosing may or may not be right for you. Some believe that they need to remain an unknown quantity or "blank slate" so that you will be free to cast them in whatever role you are comfortable with. You can look to them as a father or mother figure, or whatever else you need. Others believe that they need to be self-disclosing so that you can know them as a human being. They also have human failings; they sometimes hurt and sometimes feel angry. You will have to decide which school of thought most appeals to you.

A therapist who is self-disclosing gives you the added advantage of filling the role of a teacher in your life. He or she will not only listen to you but will also provide feedback and model healthy behavior. Only when therapists are willing to admit to their own hurts and foibles can they model healthy ways in which to deal with those difficulties. If a client will benefit from "transference"—a term that refers to casting the therapist in the role of a mother, father, or other significant person—my own experience has shown that it will occur regardless of how self-disclosing the therapist may be.

You will also want to take note of whether therapists ask you during this first session what *you* hope to get out of therapy. If they don't ask, don't hesitate to tell them anyway. You may want to inquire about the therapist's convictions regarding confidentiality. Some therapists believe that whatever a client tells them is absolutely secret, except where keeping it secret would cause them to violate mandatory reporting laws. The law in many states requires that therapists report any incidence of child abuse that you may speak about. They are also required to take unusual steps, such as committing a client to a mental health facility, if that client seems to be in imminent danger of harming himself or others.

Other therapists believe that it is in the client's best interest to share very deep concerns with the client's family members or closest friend—with or without the client's permission —especially when that person seems suicidally depressed or has exhibited other self-destructive impulses. For your own peace of mind, you may want to ask who, besides the therapist, has access to your records—a secretary, transcriptionist, partner within the practice, etc.

During one woman's first visit with a therapist, he asked whether she would mind if he allowed some of his psychology students to observe their first session together. He also informed her that he would be inviting observers into her therapy sessions from time to time. She chose not to see that particular therapist again—and rightly so.

You will want to take note of how long the therapist keeps you waiting. Although any therapist can get behind schedule on a given day, due to an emergency, a lengthy delay is worth inquiring about. If you are kept waiting for your first appointment and the therapist apologizes, explaining that he handled a crisis earlier that day, you probably won't feel the need to consider the delay too significant. If he says something like, "I always seem to be running behind, you'll get used to it," you may want to take his cavalier attitude into consideration when you make your choice.

After you begin to see a therapist regularly, if you are kept waiting once in a while you can take comfort in the fact that your therapist will allow you an extra few minutes of his or her time one day when you need it. However, if the therapist routinely keeps you waiting fifteen, twenty minutes, or more, you may reasonably question whether he or she is as dependable and emotionally available as you might wish.

Ask yourself whether your therapist returns your calls in a timely fashion, whether he or she seems to be paying close attention when you're speaking, whether you must continually remind him or her of who you are and what your reasons are for seeing him or her, and so forth. If every other consideration meets your approval, you may choose to accept a therapist's continual tardiness. That doesn't mean that you can't discuss it, however.

During your first visit, you may also want to present the therapist with a couple of hypothetical situations, based on your own history, and ask how he or she might handle that situation. You might wish to ask what attitude he or she has about touching and hugging. You may want to seek a therapist who has no objection to giving a *non-sexual* hug or to embracing you when appropriate. But you will most likely want to choose someone who has boundaries that are substantial enough that he or she always asks permission before touching a client. In fact, you may wish to establish that ground rule with everyone in your life: "No touching without permission." That's a helpful rule for those who are recovering from a violation of *any* kind.

It is never acceptable for a therapist to kiss you or to touch you in a way that causes you to feel uncomfortable. A therapist who invites you to a private lunch or dinner or expresses a wish to socialize with you privately is one you need to avoid.

As you establish an ongoing relationship with your therapist, you will probably want to take note of the ways in which he or she handles various situations. Does the therapist provide honest feedback about the way in which he or she perceives you? For instance, "Your body language and tone of voice give me the impression that you're angry, yet you're telling me that everything is 'just fine.'"

Does he or she encourage you to request honest feedback from others? Does he or she encourage you to share seemingly unrelated materials or projects? A favorite poem, art work, or piece of music—especially one you've created yourself—can provide valuable information about where you are and what you've experienced.

Does your therapist help you to set attainable goals along your path to recovery? Does he or she create an atmosphere in which you feel safe even when you "fail"? Are you afraid to admit that you may not have followed through on a plan to change a chosen behavior or on a homework assignment? If you are afraid your therapist will get mad at you or abandon you when you admit that you've failed, try to analyze where those fears are coming from. Has your therapist reacted badly to previous failures or are you reacting to "old tapes" from your past that have nothing whatever to do with him or her?

Is your therapist respectful of your defenses or does he or she try to "beat them down" in order to speed your recovery? We have developed our defenses for a reason. Trying to force our way past them often increases the length of time it takes us to recover, rather than shortening it. Our defenses will slip away as we begin to feel safe enough to face life without them. Safety is the issue. A therapist who tries to "chop" or "brow beat" through our defenses isn't likely to create an atmosphere of safety for us.

Does your therapist help you to differentiate between the need for human contact and the need for intimacy, between loving feelings and sexual feelings? Does the therapist keep his or her word? Does he or she apologize after a mistake or become defensive and unwilling to hear criticism? Does he or she allow you to express *any* emotion freely? Does your therapist help you feel safe and accepted enough to discuss absolutely anything—even if it means confessing something you're ashamed of? Do you feel you can trust him or her to whatever degree you are able to trust at this point in your recovery?

How does your therapist handle it when you get mad at him or her? Does he or she create a feeling of safety by allowing you your anger while firmly stating his or her own expectation of safety? In other words, does the therapist make it clear that it's okay to be mad at him or her, but not okay to threaten him or her with physical harm? Does he or she offer you safe alternatives for dealing with your anger—when you are angry with him or her or anyone else? Does he or she offer you guidance in discovering ways in which you may be exhibiting codependent behavior and in helping you to come up with alternatives to that sort of behavior?

Does your therapist try to help you see that you have inherent worth completely apart from your accomplishments and possessions? Does he or she listen to your opinion regarding what an event or behavior may mean? Are you encouraged to achieve a healthy independence from him or her, to find ways to nurture yourself, meet your own needs, and find your own answers whenever possible?

You will want to look for all of these qualities in a Christian therapist as well. In addition, you will want to decide whether they model a healthy dependence on God. Does he or she pray with you and offer Scripture references when they apply? Does he or she encourage you to make the Lord an integral part of your therapy? Does he or she consistently try to help you see that God is in charge of everything in your life and that "all things work together for good"?

No therapist is perfect. All we can ask is that a therapist do his or her best on our behalf. Only you can decide which of the points in this list are essential and which aren't quite so important to you personally. I would encourage you to pray before embarking on a search for a therapist. With God's help, you will find: someone who is right for you, someone you can learn to trust because he or she is trustworthy, someone who can guide you to a state of emotional health because the person has found his or her own way there. When you have found such a one, thank God for that person and forge ahead... with my prayers.

Stage-Appropriate Scriptures

IN ORDER TO REPLACE the lies we have believed with the truth, we need to know where to find the Scripture verses that will help us to successfully navigate each developmental stage. Memorizing these verses as you go through your recovery process would be extremely helpful.

Trust
Ps 13:5
Ps 37:5
Ps 56:4
Ps 125:1
Prv 3:5
Na 1:7
Rom 15:13

Autonomy
Ps 25:5
Ps 25:9
Ps 48:14
Ps 73:24
Is 30:21
Is 42:16
Jn 16:13

Initiative
Eph 4:15
1 Pt 2:2
2 Pt 1:5
2 Pt 1:6
1 Cor 13:11
Ps 92:12
Jb 17:9

Industry
Mt 5:16
Jas 2:17
Jas 2:17
Ps 34:14
1 Kgs 6:35
Heb 13:16

Identity
Rom 8:16
Ti 3:7
Jn 1:12
1 Thes 5:5
Gal 4:7
Phil 2:15
1 Jn 3:1

Intimacy
1 Cor 10:33
Rom 6:13
Rom 12:9
Rom 8:35
Jn 14:23
Jn 15:13
Jn 16:27
Jude 21
1 Jn 4:16
Dt 10:12

Notes

ONE
We Wrestle Not with Flesh and Blood

1. Lindsey, Hal, *Satan Is Alive and Well on Planet Earth* (Grand Rapids, Michigan: Zondervan Publishing House, 1972).
2. Peck, Scott, M.D., *People of the Lie* (New York, New York: Simon & Schuster, Inc., 1983).
3. Anderson, Neil T., *The Bondage Breaker* (Eugene, Oregon: Harvest House Publications, 1990), 22.
4. Neiman, Charles, *Fear: Breaking the Bondage* (El Paso, Texas: The Abundant Living Faith Center, Inc., 1986), 21.
5. Neiman, 39.

TWO
A Call to Battle

1. Quote from Eugene O'Neil from *Peter's Quotations*, Laurence J. Peter, ed. (New York, New York: William Morrow & Co., Inc., 1977), 39.

FOUR
The Nature of Our Warfare

1. Peck, 129.
2. McClung, Floyd, *The Father Heart of God* (Eugene, Oregon: Harvest House Publications, 1985), 23-24.
3. Bubeck, Mark I., *The Adversary* (Chicago, Illinois: Moody Press, 1975), 81.
4. Bubeck, 81.

SIX
Your Script

1. Festinger, L., and Carlsmith, J.M., "Cognitive Consequences of Forced

Compliance," *Journal of Abnormal and Social Psychology*, #58, 1959, 203-210.

SEVEN
Overcoming Vicious Cycles

1. Asch, S.E., "Studies of Independence and Submission in Group Pressure," *Psychological Monographs*, #416, 1956, 70.
2. Bradshaw, John, *Bradshaw On: The Family* (Pompano Beach, Florida: Health Communications, Inc., 1988), 74.

EIGHT
Frozen in Time

1. Information regarding Erikson's stage theory is taken from "Evaluating Self-Concept and Ego Development Within Erikson's Psychosocial Framework: A Formulation" by Don E. Hamacheck, *Journal of Counseling and Development*, Vol. 66, No. 8, April 1988, 354-360.

NINE
The Need to Be Needed

1. Beattie, Melody, *Co-Dependent No More* (New York, New York: Hazelden Books, Harper Collins Pub., 1987), 31.
2. *Sober Times—The Recovery Magazine*, San Diego, Nov. 1991, 2-3.

TWELVE
Ritualized Abuse

1. Kahaner, Larry, *Cults That Kill* (New York, New York: Warner Books, Inc., 1988), 90.
2. Kahaner, 129.
3. Kahaner, 71.
4. Kahaner, 239.
5. Efron, Sonni, "Forced to Kill the Baby," *L.A. Times*, Orange County edition, March 21, 1991, B1.
6. Segal, Julius, *Winning Life's Toughest Battles* (McGraw-Hill, 1986), 55.

Other Books of Interest
from Servant Publications

A Woman's Guide to Spiritual Warfare
Quin Sherrer and Ruthanne Garlock

Women everywhere face battles that threaten to overwhelm them and those they love. *A Woman's Guide to Spiritual Warfare* shows how they can work with God to change the course of their lives and the lives of family and friends. Quin Sherrer and Ruthanne Garlock help readers recognize the tremendous spiritual power God offers them to resist the enemy.

Whether women like it or not, there *is* a war going on, and God has given them places in the battle. This book calls readers to take their place with confidence. **$8.99**

The Believer's Guide to Spiritual Warfare
Wising Up to Satan's Influence in Your World
Thomas B. White

As an expert in the field of spiritual warfare, Tom White has equipped thousands of men and women to discern and combat demonic forces in their world. *The Believer's Guide to Spiritual Warfare* offers biblically sound, accurate, and balanced teaching on the unseen war being waged around us.

Complete with real-life illustrations, sample prayers, proven techniques, and answers to the most commonly asked questions about warfare, this book will help believers to fulfill a central call of the gospel—to resist evil with the power and authority of the cross. **$8.99**